SILVER BOOK BOX

NOT MANY PEOPLE KNOW THAT!

Silver Book Box
Series Editor: Julia Eccleshare

SILVER BOOK BOX

NOT MANY PEOPLE KNOW THAT!

Michael Caine's Almanac of Amazing Information

All royalties to the National Playing Fields Association

**MACMILLAN
EDUCATION**

Complete text
First published by Robson Books 1984

First published by Macmillan Education in abridged form 1988

Published by
MACMILLAN EDUCATION LTD
Houndmills, Basingstoke, Hampshire RG21 2XS
and London
Companies and representatives
throughout the world

Series designer Julian Holland

Cartoons by Brian Walker

Cover illustration: All Action Photographic

Typeset by Vine & Gorfin Ltd, Exmouth, Devon

Printed in Hong Kong

British Library Cataloguing in Publication Data
Caine, Michael
Not many people know that!: Michael Caine's
almanac of amazing information.—Abridged
—(Silver book box).
1. Curiosities and wonders
I. Title II. Series
032′.02   AG243
ISBN 0-333-45301-8

The author's royalty is donated to
the National Playing Fields Association

January

1 January

Idi Amin, who became one of the most ruthless tyrants in the world, was born on 1 January 1928. Early in his life, Amin served in the British Army, and was a noted Rugby player.

John Paul Getty, once the richest man in the world, had a payphone in his huge mansion.

When public toilets were first installed in England in 1852, the cost of 'spending a penny' was tuppence.

2 January

One of Britain's most famous composers was born today in 1905. Sir Michael Tippett's pieces are very difficult to play. For instance, during his Second Symphony, the orchestra got lost in the middle of the piece and the conductor had to go back to the beginning and start again.

Chop-suey is not a native Chinese dish. It was invented by Chinese immigrants in California.

The Hundred Years War lasted 116 years.

3 January

On 3 January 1892, J. R. R. Tolkien was born. His famous book *Lord of the Rings* has sold over three million copies and has been translated into nine languages.

The sun's mass decreases by four million tons per second.

Judy Garland's false eyelashes were sold at auction in 1979 for US $125.

4 January

The famous midget, 'General Tom Thumb', was born on this day back in 1838. Though he came from a normal family, he stopped growing at the age of six months. His final height was a mere forty inches.

Greenland is the largest island in the world. It is about ten times the size of the whole of Great Britain.

The correct name for a group of crows is a 'murder'.

5 January

For Roman Catholics, 5 January is St Simeon Stylites' Day. He was a fifth-century hermit who showed his devotion to God by spending years sitting on top of a flagpole.

According to the laws of science, the bumble-bee shouldn't be able to fly.

Worms are all both male and female – they have both sets of sexual organs on their bodies.

6 January

Richard II was born today in 1367. When he died in 1400, a hole was left in the side of his tomb so that people could touch his royal head.

The Guiness Book of Records has broken a record of its own – it is the book which is most often stolen from British Public Libraries.

There are more bacteria in a hospital operating theatre than there are in an ordinary living-room.

7 January

On 7 January 1904, the 'CQD' distress signal was introduced, 'CQ' standing for 'Seek You' with a 'D' for 'Danger' added. It only lasted for a couple of years before 'SOS' took over in 1906.

Sir Winston Churchill wrote a number of film scripts.

John Glenn, the American astronaut who carried out the first manned orbit of the earth, was showered with 3474 tons of ticker-tape when he got back.

8 January

On 8 January 1935, Elvis Presley was born. It is estimated that he has received over eighty gold discs (one million sales each time) worldwide.

If you got rid of all the space in the atoms which go to make up a camel, you could pass a camel through the eye of a needle.

9 January

The amount of carbon in the human body is enough to fill about nine thousand lead pencils.

The Forth railway bridge in Scotland is a metre longer in the summer than in the winter.

Pope Adrian VI died after a fly got stuck in his throat as he was taking a drink from a water fountain.

10 January

Franklin D. Roosevelt, the only US President to be elected three times, had polio.

The song which is sung most often in the world – 'Happy Birthday to You' – is still under copyright. This runs out in 2010.

11 January

Thomas Hardy, the English poet and novelist, died on 11 January 1928. His ashes were buried in Westminster Abbey, but his heart was removed and placed in the grave of his beloved first wife in Stinsford Churchyard.

Handel wrote the score of his *Messiah* in just over three weeks.

The *Mona Lisa* was originally bought by Francis I of France in 1517 to hang in his bathroom. The painting is now valued at over £35 million.

12 January

On 12 January 1948, the first full-size supermarket to be built in Britain received its grand opening, at Manor Park. It was called 'The London Co-op'.

In winter, the skating rinks in the parks of Moscow cover more than 250 000 square metres of land.

The hydrochloric acid in the human digestive system is strong enough to dissolve a nail.

13 January

The Marx Brothers (Chico, Harpo, Groucho, and Zeppo) were actually named respectively Leonard, Adolph, Julius and Herbert.

The background radiation in Aberdeen is twice that of the rest of Great Britain.

Ethelred the Unready, King of England in the tenth century, was found on his wedding night in bed with both his wife and his mother-in-law.

14 January

When Humphrey Bogart died on 14 January 1957, his wife Lauren Bacall placed a gold whistle inside his coffin. The inscription on the whistle read: 'If you need anything, just whistle', which is a line from their first film together, *To Have and Have Not*.

Turtles, as a species, are about 275 million years old.

15 January

On this day in 1867, there was a very severe frost in London. Over forty people died when the ice broke on the main lake in Regent's Park.

The Angel Falls in Venezuela are nearly twenty times taller than the Niagara Falls.

Three-fifths of all species of mammals are rodents.

16 January

On 16 January 1920 the USA prohibited the public sale of alcohol. The reaction was 'bootlegging', which got its name from the cowboys' old method of hiding alcohol in their boots when selling it illegally to the Indians.

There are about ten times as many sheep in Australia as there are human beings.

The phrase, 'The Three Rs', standing for 'reading, writing, and arithmetic', was coined by Sir William Curtis, who was illiterate.

17 January

Benjamin Franklin, who helped to write the American Declaration of Independence, was born on this day in 1706. One of his greatest achievements was the invention of the rocking-chair.

About two-thirds of the world's population do not use newspapers, television, radio, or telephone.

An elephant's trunk can hold one-and-a-half gallons of water.

18 January

Cary Grant, one of Hollywood's most successful actors, was born in Bristol, England on 18 January 1904. He was always evasive about his true age. When a journalist sent him a telegram asking: 'How old Cary Grant?', he replied 'Old Cary Grant fine. How you?'

'The' is the most used word in the English language followed by 'of' and 'and'.

19 January

James Watt, who perfected the idea of the steam engine, was born today in 1736. He suffered severe migraines throughout his life.

Oxygen molecules travel at roughly the same speed as a jet aircraft.

Only female mosquitoes bite.

20 January

The most common surname in France is 'Martin'.

Walt Disney himself did the original voice for the cartoon character, Mickey Mouse.

St Nicholas, the original Father Christmas, is patron saint of thieves, virgins and Communist Russia.

A shark has to keep moving forward in order to live.

21 January

Lenin, the great Russian leader, died on this day in 1924. He suffered from a brain illness late in his life, and, by the time of his death, his brain was a quarter of its normal size.

Some parts of Paris have public flush toilets for dogs.

A greenfly born on a Sunday can become a grandparent by the following Wednesday.

22 January

Queen Victoria died on 22 January 1901. Among her many claims to fame, she was the first person ever to use chloroform against pain in childbirth.

There is no mention of cats in the Bible.

The amount spent on advertising Coca-Cola over the years is equivalent to providing every family in the world with one free bottle.

23 January

Humphrey Bogart was born today in 1899, although his film company, Warner Brothers, claimed that he was born on Christmas Day in order to romanticise his image.

Some Eskimos use refrigerators to keep their food from freezing.

Your body contains enough iron to make a spike strong enough to hold your weight.

24 January

Frederick the Great, King of Prussia, was born on 24 January 1712. He became a great military commander, as well as something of an eccentric. For example, he often had his coffee made with champagne instead of water.

One of Queen Victoria's wedding gifts was a half-ton cheese, which was over three metres in diameter.

The average person has fewer than two legs.

25 January

In *The Wizard of Oz*, the scene in which Judy Garland sings 'Over the Rainbow' was originally cut because the producers thought it too slow, contributing little to the plot. It was only restored at the last minute.

Catgut does not come from cats, but is made from the intestines of sheep.

Ice is lighter than water.

26 January

On this day in 1905, Captain Wells discovered the famous Cullinan diamond at the Premier mine in South Africa. It still ranks as the largest diamond ever found in the world, weighing over one-and-a-quarter pounds.

Crocodiles are colour-blind.

It would take about two million hydrogen atoms to cover the average-sized full stop.

27 January

To make just one pound of honey, bees must collect nectar from over two million separate flowers.

Not all dinosaurs were huge and frightening: in fact some were as small as chickens.

28 January

Cats cannot taste sugar.

In 1849, David Atchison became President of the US for just one day, and he spent most of the day asleep.

There are two miles of passages in the Houses of Parliament.

29 January

The eye of a giant squid is larger than a person's head.

The US has a marriage bureau to help find suitable partners for lonely cats and dogs.

The biggest fish and chip shop in the world is Harry Ramsden's in Yorkshire.

30 January

Gandhi was assassinated on 30 January 1948. As he was dying, Gandhi turned to his murderer and gave him the Hindu sign of forgiveness.

The two highest IQs ever recorded (on a standard test) both belonged to women.

The ordinary house-fly beats its wings nearly two hundred times a second.

31 January

Franz Schubert, the composer, was born on this day in 1797. He was a very poor man, and many of his compositions were first tried out over a drink with friends in his local tavern.

Over two thousand pints of beer are drunk in the House of Commons every week.

Biscuits get their name from two French words, *bis cuit*, which mean 'twice cooked'. The original biscuits had to be preserved for long periods and had to be cooked twice to make them last as long as possible.

February

1 February

The film-star Clark Gable was born today in 1901. He received a medal for a series of daring bomber missions during the Second World War, and reached the rank of Major.

You have to frown nearly a quarter of a million times to make one wrinkle.

Snails can sleep for three years without waking up.

2 February

Kangaroos are only one inch long at birth.

Although Cleopatra is often supposed to have died after a bite from an asp, the species does not exist in Egypt.

3 February

Sir Winston Churchill was born in a ladies' cloakroom, after his mother went into labour during a dance at Blenheim Palace.

The 'Crystal Palace', at the Great Exhibition of 1851, contained one million square feet of glass and was visited by over six million people.

The English language contains about 490 000 words (excluding some 300 000 technical terms).

4 February

This day in 1962 was a Sunday, and saw the appearance of the first-ever colour magazine supplement. It was produced by *The Sunday Times*.

Half of the world's area of land-water is in Canada.

5 February

Sir Robert Peel, who was born on this day in 1788, was the founder of the Metropolitan Police Force in London. His name is remembered in the nickname commonly given to police constables, 'bobbies'.

The Sun makes up over ninety-nine per cent of the solar system's weight.

6 February

Queen Elizabeth II came to the Throne today back in 1952, after the death of her father George VI. Many important world figures are entertained at Buckingham Palace each year, and place-settings at meals are measured with a ruler.

Whales can't swim backwards.

Fifty-pence coins have a life-expectancy of around fifty years.

7 February

On this day in 1837, Florence Nightingale claimed she had a vision of God. God told her to renounce her rich social background and take up a mission in life. A few years later she took up nursing.

One gallon of fuel moves the QE2 six inches.

The average British family uses two miles of toilet paper a year.

8 February

The surface area of one human lung is equal to that of a tennis court.

An octopus has three hearts.

Every British Post Office is given a small grant towards the upkeep of a cat. They are meant to be used as mice-catchers.

9 February

On 9 February 1942, soap-rationing began in Britain.

Since 1959, more than six thousand pieces of space-machinery have fallen out of orbit – many of these have hit the earth's surface.

The longest kiss in the history of Hollywood came in the 1941 film, *You're in the Army Now*. Reginald Toomey and Jane Wyman were locked together for three minutes and five seconds.

10 February

The American swimmer, Mark Spitz, was born on this day in 1950. In the 1972 Olympics, he won four individual gold medals, and was a member of three winning relay-teams. All seven of his victories also resulted in world records.

Some soft drinks are made sweeter by adding coal.

You use forty-three muscles to frown, and only seventeen to smile.

11 February

Because metal was scarce, the Oscars given out during the Second World War were made of wood.

In Ancient China, people committed suicide by consuming a pound of salt.

Dogs sweat through the pads of their feet.

12 February

Abraham Lincoln was born today in 1809. During the American Civil War, the King of Siam offered him the use of his official war-elephants. Lincoln declined the offer.

Only two words in the English language end in the letters 'shion' – 'cushion' and 'fashion'.

During the reign of Elizabeth I, there was a tax put on men's beards.

13 February

People in Siberia usually buy their milk frozen on a stick.

The state-flag of Alaska was designed by a thirteen-year-old boy.

The kiwi is the only bird with nostrils at the end of its bill.

14 February

In 1929, members of Al Capone's gang killed seven unarmed men, because they were part of 'Bugs' Moran's rival gang. The event became known as the St Valentine's Day Massacre. The killers surprised their victims by dressing up as policemen.

A sloth can move twice as fast through water as it can on dry land.

Spain literally means 'the land of rabbits'.

15 February

A snail can have about twenty-five thousand teeth.

The moon is four hundred times smaller than the sun, but it is also four hundred times nearer to the earth. That is why there can be a perfect eclipse.

A large-sized whale needs at least three tons of food a day.

16 February

Giraffes are not able to cough.

We eat an average of one-hundred-and-forty-thousand pounds of food in our lifetime.

Many sailors used to wear gold earrings so that they could always afford a proper burial when they died.

17 February

Geronimo, the great Apache leader, died today in 1908. Late in his life he joined the Dutch Reformed Church, but was thrown out for gambling.

Spiders' webs are traditionally a natural clotting agent. If they are applied to a cut, they are meant to stop the flow of blood, and help it to heal quickly.

A Boeing 707 uses four thousand gallons of fuel to reach the top of its take-off climb.

18 February

On this day in 1965, Gambia became independent. It is the smallest nation on the African continent, and its official language is English.

By the time you have read this sentence, you will have been bombarded by air molecules more than one hundred billion billion times.

Whatever its size or thickness, no piece of paper can be folded in half more than seven times.

19 February

Charles Blondin, the greatest tightrope-walker of his age, and the first man to cross the Niagara Falls on a three-inch rope, died today in 1897. He once walked across the Falls with his agent on his back.

Approximately four million people attended the open-air funeral of President Nasser of Egypt.

The French eat about five hundred million snails a year.

20 February

Ralph and Carolyn Cummins had five children between 1952 and 1966. All five were born on the same day – today.

St John the Evangelist was the only one of the Twelve Apostles to die a natural death.

The Swiss are the world's biggest consumers of cheese, per person.

21 February

Sir Winston Churchill rationed himself to fifteen cigars a day.

Only male canaries can sing.

During the chariot scene in *Ben Hur*, a small red car can be seen driving by in the distance.

22 February

When you blush, your stomach-lining also becomes redder.

The children's nursery rhyme, 'Ring-a-Ring-Roses', actually refers to the Black Death, which killed around thirty million people in the fourteenth century.

When the volcano Krakatoa erupted in 1883, the sound was heard in Texas, USA.

23 February

At their nearest point, Russia and America are only two miles apart.

The yo-yo originated in the Philippines, where it was used as a weapon in hunting.

Hindus do not like dying in bed. They prefer to come to rest beside a river.

24 February

There are more kinds of insects in the world than all kinds of other animals put together.

If our ears were only slightly more sensitive, we would hear molecules colliding in the air.

25 February

There is only one bird which can fly backwards – the humming-bird.

The word 'denim' was invented because the fabric originally came from the French city of Nîmes. It was therefore labelled 'de Nîmes'.

It is thought that some unborn babies dream.

26 February

Polar bears can run at speeds of up to twenty-five miles an hour.

In the north of Norway, the sun shines day and night for three-and-a-half months each summer.

The human nervous system can relay messages to and from the brain at speeds of up to two hundred miles an hour.

27 February

The English actress Elizabeth Taylor was born in London on this day in 1929. The highly expensive film *Cleopatra*, in which she took the leading role, was banned in Egypt in 1963 because she was a Jewish convert.

The population of the world could fit on to the Isle of Wight, though there would be standing-room only.

28 February

The American novelist Henry James died on this day in 1916. An extensive traveller, he suffered from constipation for much of his life.

The country Brazil got its name from its native Brazil-nut tree, and not the other way round.

Bees have five eyes.

29 February

Until the 1930s, 29 February was the feast of St Oswald of Worcester. Then someone decided that St Oswald was missing out by having his feast-day only once every four years, so it was moved to 28 February.

The hippopotamus is born under water.

About one-quarter of the world's population lives in China.

March

1 March

Pauline Masters, widely held to be the shortest person of all time, died today in 1895, at a height of only twenty-three inches. Her death at 19 was largely caused by an excess of alcohol.

Whales increase in weight thirty thousand million times in their first two years.

All the planets in our solar system could fit inside a hollow Jupiter.

2 March

On this day in 1972, the spaceship *Pioneer 10* took off to go further than any previous spaceship, and break out of our own solar system. It reached the moon in under half a day, and is expected to continue travelling for another two million years.

A South African monkey survived trench warfare during the First World War, and so was awarded a medal and promoted to the rank of corporal.

People in Tibet stick their tongues out at each other as a sign of respect.

3 March

Alexander Graham Bell, the inventor of the telephone, was born on 3 March 1824. Neither his mother nor his wife would have been able to reap the benefits however, because both of them were deaf.

A python is able both to eat a pig whole, but also to fast for over a year at a time.

Only one-twentieth of all children are born on the day predicted by doctors.

4 March

Marlon Brando was born on this day in 1924. He was once quoted as saying: 'An actor's a guy who, if you ain't talking about him, ain't listening.'

Crocodiles carry their young in their mouths.

The nerve fibres in the body of the giant squid are five hundred times thicker than our own.

5 March

The Russian leader Stalin died on 5 March 1953. He suffered from having one arm longer than the other and a face scarred by a dose of smallpox.

Blank ammunition worth over £20 000 per year is used in Britain for purely ceremonial purposes.

The largest carnivorous mammal in the world is the Alaskan brown bear.

Sloths spend over seventy-five per cent of their lives asleep.

6 March

Human beings are the only animals capable of smiling.

There are more people in Monaco's State Symphony Orchestra than there are in its Army.

A giraffe's neck contains the same number of vertebrae as a human's.

An average of over ten people a year are killed by lightning in Britain alone.

7 March

In Moscow, over 45000 people attend the theatre and concert halls every day.

Twenty thousand people attended the public cremation of Dr William Price, who was a leading nineteenth-century campaigner for the right of people to be cremated.

8 March

King William III of England died on 8 March 1702. He had been thrown from his horse a few days earlier, after it had tripped over a molehill.

The first pancakes and the first pancake-races were invented to use up stocks of food that were banned during Lent.

9 March

Ernest Bevin, the Minister of Labour in Britain during the Second World War, was born today in 1881. His education, however, was short – he left school at the tender age of eleven.

Many male fishes blow bubbles when they want to attract a female.

About seventy per cent of the living organisms in the world are bacteria.

10 March

In Britain, more money is spent on cigarettes and alcohol than on life insurance.

The Russian composer Borodin was also a Professor of Chemistry.

11 March

The book *Aircraft Recognition* by F. A. Saville-Smith, published in 1941, has sold over seven million copies.

The Crusaders had difficulty in transporting corpses off the battlefield for proper burial. So they carried with them huge cauldrons for boiling the bodies. Bones were much lighter and easier to carry.

12 March

President Kaunda of Zambia once threatened to resign if his fellow countrymen didn't stop drinking so much alcohol. The President himself was teetotal.

Over half the men in Corfu are called Spiro.

The only wild camels in the world are to be found in Australia.

13 March

The planet Uranus has only been known for two hundred years. It was discovered by Sir William Herschel on 13 March 1781.

The lance ceased to be an official battle weapon in the British Army in 1927.

The streets and parks of London are subjected to over one hundred thousand gallons of urine per day.

14 March

Albert Einstein was born on 14 March 1879. Unfortunately his final words are lost to posterity. The nurse who was looking after him when he died did not understand German.

The smallest trees in the world are the dwarf willows of Greenland. They are about two inches tall.

A mosquito has forty-seven teeth.

15 March

Julius Caesar was murdered on this day in 44 BC. It is said that the reason he always wore a laurel wreath was because he did not want anyone to know that he was going bald.

Since the turn of the century in America, every successfully-elected President has been taller than his rival candidate.

More fish and chips are sold at Labour Party conferences than at those held by the Conservatives.

16 March

Aubrey Beardsley was one of the most influential artists and illustrators of the last century. However, his working life lasted only six years, and he died on 16 March 1898 at the age of twenty-five.

During the seventeenth century, the Sultan of Turkey ordered the drowning of his entire harem of women. He then promptly created a new one.

17 March

This is St Patrick's Day, named for the patron saint of Ireland. Though his history is rather confused, there is one thing we can be sure of – St Patrick was not Irish.

A group of toads is called a 'knot'.

Fillings in people's teeth have been known to pick up radio waves.

18 March

An electric eel produces an average of four hundred volts.

The underwater explorer Jacques Cousteau invented the aqualung while serving with the French Resistance during the Second World War.

19 March

Sergei Diaghilev, the 'father of modern ballet', was born on this day in 1872. His original ambition was to be a composer of classical music, but he was advised against this by the famous Russian musician Rimsky-Korsakov.

Within a pride of lions, ninety per cent of the hunting is done by the females.

Paper was invented early in the second century by a Chinese eunuch.

20 March

The Amazon River has over a thousand tributary streams.

If all the water in the oceans of the world were evenly distributed among us each person would receive over one hundred billion gallons of water.

During the nineteenth century, tomato ketchup was sold as a medicine.

21 March

Johann Sebastian Bach was born on 21 March 1685. He came from an extraordinarily musical family, with over fifty of his relatives pursuing a career in music.

Bamboo can grow over one metre in the space of twenty-four hours.

A cheetah can reach a speed of forty-five miles an hour, from a standing start, in two seconds.

Admiral Lord Nelson was only five feet two inches tall.

22 March

Sir Winston Churchill had such an amazing memory that he could recite an entire Shakespeare play correctly.

Fewer than a quarter of the inhabitants of India can speak the country's official language of Hindi.

23 March

The three largest circulation daily newspapers in the world are all Russian.

The Russian revolutionary Leon Trotsky once appeared in a Hollywood silent movie as an extra.

Fourteen million people died during the First World War. Twenty million people died in a 'flu epidemic just afterwards.

24 March

Catherine I of Russia made it a rule that no man was allowed to get drunk at her parties before nine o'clock.

Gold is the sixteenth most rare chemical element.

The Ancient Egyptians trained baboons to wait at their tables.

25 March

On 25 March 1964 the British Government set aside an acre of the famous turf at Runnymede, where the Magna Carta was signed, as a memorial to the late John F. Kennedy.

Every cubic mile of seawater contains an average of one hundred and fifty million tons of minerals.

A flush toilet was found in the palace at Knossos. The city dates back to 2000 BC.

26 March

The great French actress Sarah Berhardt died on 26 March 1923. She had one of her legs amputated in 1915, but continued to act until her death, playing roles specifically created to suit her disability.

Men have an average of ten per cent more red blood cells than women.

The Sahara Desert is as large as America.

27 March

King James I of England died on 27 March 1625. After Sir Walter Raleigh had introduced tobacco to England, King James wrote what might be called the first Government health warning – a booklet condemning smoking as dangerous and anti-social.

The speed of the earth's rotation at its fastest point (the equator) is about one thousand miles per hour.

There are over ten thousand golf courses in the USA.

28 March

In the last hundred years, there have been four natural disasters on 28 March. In 1888 Wellington, New Zealand was struck by a devastating tidal wave; in 1920 a tornado hit Chicago, USA, causing over a million pounds' worth of damage; in 1965 an earthquake devastated Chile, and five years later another hit western Turkey, killing over one thousand people.

Gorillas often sleep for up to fourteen hours a day.

29 March

The male Californian sea-otter grips the nose of the female with his teeth during mating.

Princess Anne was the only competitor at the 1976 Montreal Olympics who did not have to undergo a sex test.

An approaching car has a shriller noise than one going away.

30 March

Over half the people in Great Britain enter the Football Pools every week.

Lions are exported to Africa by Windsor Safari Park in England.

At the height of German inflation in the 1920s, one US dollar was worth 4 000 000 000 000 000 000 marks.

31 March

The average porcupine has over 30 000 quills.

When he was young and impoverished, Pablo Picasso kept warm by burning his own paintings.

The youngest Nobel prize-winner ever was called William Bragg. When he was only twenty-three he shared the physics prize with his father.

April

1 April

On this day in 1954, Mrs P. Ride, a mother of five, took out the historic patent on sliced bread.

It took two weeks for Europe to learn of President Lincoln's death, proving that even the most important news does not always travel fast.

The second most common atom to hydrogen is not oxygen, as you might expect, but helium.

2 April

Charlemagne, the first Holy Roman Emperor, was born today in about 742. He was described as a giant, for in an age when the average height was well below that of today, he is said to have been over seven feet tall.

Even the smallest volcano exerts more power than the largest earthquake or hurricane.

Ninety-nine per cent of all the forms of life that have ever existed on the earth are now extinct.

3 April

Washington Irving, the American writer and historian, was born on this day in 1783. He found the idea for the character Rip Van Winkle in the legend of the Cretan poet, Epimenides, who decided to take a short nap while out hunting, and did not wake up for fifty years.

John D. Rockefeller gave away over five hundred million dollars during his lifetime.

In California, it is illegal to kill or threaten a butterfly.

4 April

The American Civil Rights leader, Martin Luther King, was assassinated on 4 April 1968. Back in 1941, when he was only twelve years old, Dr King became so depressed that he twice attempted suicide by jumping out of his bedroom window.

Lightning is essential to the survival of plant life on this planet, because the intense heat it generates when it hits our air supply transforms nitrogen into the nitrates which feed plants.

5 April

On 5 April 1955, Sir Winston Churchill resigned as Prime Minister of Great Britain. And on exactly the same day twenty-one years later, Prime Minister Harold Wilson announced his decision to step down.

The southernmost tip of Africa is not the Cape of Good Hope, as most people think, but Cape Agulhas.

Hedgehogs couldn't survive without fleas, because fleas provide essential stimulation to their skin.

6 April

Because whales have fixed eyeballs they have to move their whole body in order to shift their line of vision.

In the two years after the first 'talkie' film appeared, American cinemas attracted over one hundred million people a week.

At the centre of the sun, the temperature can be as high as twenty million degrees Centigrade.

7 April

According to a tradition dating back to the sixth century, the first cuckoo of the year appears on 7 April at a town called St Brynach in Wales.

The Palace of Versailles in France has over a thousand fountains scattered around its grounds.

'Mummies' are so-called because of the wax (called 'mum') which is smeared on to the bandages for waterproofing.

8 April

The city of Damascus has been inhabited ever since 2000 BC.

Marie Curie, who twice won the Nobel Prize, and discovered radium, was not allowed to become a member of the famous French Academy – because she was a woman.

9 April

Lenin's real name was Vladimir Ilyich Ulyanov, but Lenin was not his only pseudonym. He used one hundred and fifty others.

The original name for the United Nations was the 'Associated Powers'.

Over two hundred different languages are spoken throughout the Soviet Union.

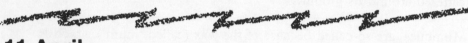

10 April

On 10 April 1932, Paul Von Hindenburg was re-elected as President of Germany. He won nineteen million votes. Hitler, as Chancellor, won thirteen million.

Only one American President has been a bachelor – James Buchanan.

11 April

John Merrick, the 'Elephant Man', died on this day in 1890. His name came from the disease called elephantiasis, which causes some parts of the body to swell up. His head was so large that he had to sleep with it resting on his knees, and it was probably the weight of it which dislocated his neck and caused his death.

There are more Jews in America than in the whole of the state of Israel.

25 December was not celebrated as the birthday of Jesus Christ until AD 440.

There are more miles of canals in Birmingham than there are in Venice.

12 April

Harry S. Truman became President of America on this day in 1945. The initial 'S' in the middle of his name does not, in fact, mean anything. Both his grandfathers had names beginning with 'S', and so Truman's mother did not want to disappoint either of them.

The Pacific Ocean covers nearly half the globe.

13 April

Thre are over five thousand islands in the group called the Philippines.

New York City passed a law in 1978 which requires dog-owners to clean up after their pets or face a fine.

The water in the Dead Sea is so salty that it is far easier to float than to drown.

14 April

President Abraham Lincoln was assassinated on 14 April 1865 by the actor John Wilkes Booth. Booth was so nervous before the event that he consumed at least one bottle of spirits during the hours leading up to the shooting at 10.15 p.m. His accomplice, who was meant to shoot Vice-President Andrew Johnson, became too drunk to fire.

Louis Braille, who invented the Braille system of reading for the blind, was himself blind from the age of three.

15 April

On 15 April 1912 the SS *Titanic* sank on her maiden voyage and over 1500 people died. Fourteen years earlier a novel was published by Morgan Robertson which seemed to foretell the disaster. The book described a ship the same size as the *Titanic* which crashes into an iceberg on its maiden voyage on a misty April night. The name of Robertson's fictional ship was the *Titan*.

Frank Sinatra was once quoted as saying that rock 'n' roll was only played by 'cretinous goons'.

16 April

Madame Tussaud, whose waxworks are one of the popular tourist attractions in London, died today in 1850. During the French Revolution her model-making skills were employed in making death masks for the victims of the dreaded guillotine.

Holland is the most densely-populated country in the world, with over a thousand people per square mile.

Americans spend four times as much per year on pet food as they do on baby food.

17 April

The Budget speech of this day in 1956 saw the introduction of Premium Savings Bonds into Britain. The machine which picks the winning numbers is called ERNIE, an acronym standing for 'Electronic Random Number Indicator Equipment'.

The symptoms of haemophilia are never displayed by women, but only they can pass it on.

For reasons of security, only people who were illiterate were considered for more routine jobs at the first atomic bomb construction centre in New Mexico.

Following Aristotle, the scientists of the Middle Ages believed that the heart – and not the brain – was the seat of human intelligence.

Honey is used to fill the centres of golf balls.

19 April

One in eight people in the world today suffers from chronic malnutrition.

Opium was used widely as a painkiller during the American Civil War. As a result, over one hundred thousand soldiers had become drug-addicts by the end of the war.

Half the world lives in just four countries – China, Russia, America and India. The other half is spread over the remaining one-hundred-and-sixty countries.

20 April

The name given to the atomic bomb is rather misleading, because almost any explosion involves an atomic reaction. The atomic bomb involves a nuclear reaction.

There is apparently a higher density of ghosts in Britain than in any other country.

21 April

Lightning is more likely than not to strike the same place twice, because it follows the path of least resistance.

There are more cars than people in Los Angeles.

Every year the Isles of Scilly send sixty million flowers (mostly daffodils) to be sold in London's New Covent Garden flower market.

22 April

When she was sentenced to death by King Henry VIII, Anne Boleyn chose decapitation in preference to the more usual punishment for her crime, of being burnt at the stake.

23 April

Two of the greatest writers who have ever lived, William Shakespeare and Miguel de Cervantes (who wrote *Don Quixote*), both died on 23 April 1616.

In 1647 the English Parliament abolished Christmas.

Before the custom was stopped by the British, Indian women used to be burnt alive on their husband's funeral pyre. This was called *suttee*.

24 April

The English novelist Anthony Trollope was born today in 1815. He also invented the pillar-box.

During the nineteenth century, it was possible to travel all the way from Scotland to Jerusalem by the old Roman roads, pausing only to make the two necessary sea-crossings.

25 April

In 1870 there were twice as many books on religion published as there were novels.

Molluscs are second only to insects as the most numerous living creatures on earth.

26 April

In the seventeenth century nearly sixty million people are thought to have died in Europe from smallpox.

Because it is so small, a humming-bird must eat constantly or risk death by starvation in a matter of hours.

If the entire history of the earth so far were to be compressed into one calendar year, then humans made their first appearance less than an hour ago.

27 April

During the 1970s, Thomas Hardy was the most popular English-language author in Japan.

Sir Isaac Newton was only twenty-three years old when he discovered the law of gravity.

28 April

Coffee is the second largest item of international commerce in the world. The largest is petrol.

The poison cyanide is present in apple pips, but only in small doses.

29 April

Sir Thomas Beecham, the English composer and conductor, was born on 29 April 1879. He was once quoted as saying: 'Why do we have all these third-rate foreign conductors around – when we have so many second-rate ones of our own?'

There was a fall of black snow in Sweden in 1969.

The Great Wall of China took 1700 years to build.

30 April

Adolf Hitler committed suicide in a Berlin bunker on 30 April 1945. During his time in power in Germany it was illegal for a policeman to call his dog Adolf.

A koala bear can survive by eating only the leaves of the eucalyptus tree.

The two men who started the California Gold Rush – Sutter and
· Marshall – did not find much gold themselves, and both died poor.

May

1 May

The French chemist Louis Pasteur, who pioneered the idea of pasteurisation, was obsessive about his own hygiene, and often refused to shake hands with people.

Water freezes faster if cooled quickly from a warm temperature, than it does from a colder one.

Over three-quarters of a potato is water.

2 May

A fully-loaded supertanker travelling at normal speed takes at least twenty minutes to stop.

In the English hospitals of the seventeenth century, children were entitled to two gallons of beer as part of their weekly diet.

In 1979 snow fell on the Sahara Desert for the first time in living memory.

3 May

Benito Mussolini, the Italian dictator, welcomed Adolf Hitler to Rome on this day in 1938 to mark the start of their military alliance. Mussolini was a difficult child at school. He was eventually expelled for stabbing a fellow pupil in the buttocks.

The English historian and theologian the Venerable Bede, was, more than anyone else, the person who popularised the dating of events according to the BC/AD system.

4 May

The world's tallest building, the Sears Tower in Chicago, was finally 'topped off' on 4 May 1974. It has the same number of storeys as its closest rival, The World Trade Center (110), but at 1454 feet, it is 104 feet higher.

Men outnumber women in prisons by over thirty to one.

Iceland is the world's oldest functioning democracy.

5 May

In the early seventeenth century, over a thousand European children were kidnapped and shipped to the USA to become slaves.

The scene where the king is deposed in Shakespeare's *Richard II* was never allowed to be performed during the reign of Elizabeth I.

6 May

The heart of Archbishop Cranmer was found intact amongst the ashes after he was burnt at the stake.

One person's skin weighs a total of about six pounds.

Adolf Hitler's cook was Jewish.

7 May

If all the gold produced in the world in the last five centuries were to be melted down and compressed, it could be made into a cube measuring fifty feet each side.

The largest egg in the world is the ostrich egg – it takes about forty minutes to hard-boil completely.

8 May

There are over one million tubes in the human kidney.

President Abraham Lincoln died believing he was illegitimate – but he was mistaken.

Only one person walked beside Mozart's coffin as it made its way to the cemetery where he was buried in an unmarked pauper's grave.

9 May

Eau de Cologne was originally marketed as a protection against the plague.

All Sikhs take the name of 'Singh', meaning 'Lion-hearted'.

The only Shakespearian play which does not contain at least one song is *The Comedy of Errors*.

10 May

The American dancer Fred Astaire was born on 10 May 1899. He was thought so valuable by his film studio that they insured his legs for $650 000.

The largest cell in the human body is the female reproductive cell, the ovum. The smallest is the male sperm.

If you travel from east to west across the Soviet Union, you will cross seven time-zones.

11 May

Irving Berlin, who was born on 11 May 1888 and who composed three thousand songs in his lifetime, could not read music.

Astronauts in orbit around the earth can see the wakes produced by ships.

Most people have lost fifty per cent of their taste buds by the time they reach the age of sixty.

12 May

The British did not release the body of Napoleon Bonaparte to the French until twenty days after his death.

The human body contains about sixty thousand miles of blood vessels.

Cancer claims forty victims an hour in America.

13 May

King Ptolemy IV of Egypt had a passion for large rowing boats. The biggest one needed ten thousand oarsmen to propel it through the water.

Sir Winston Churchill's mother was descended from a Red Indian.

14 May

Israel, proclaimed an independent state on 14 May 1948, has the highest military spending per capita of any country in the world.

Pablo Picasso was abandoned by the midwife just after his birth because she thought he was stillborn. He was saved by an uncle.

The power of the first hydrogen bomb, tested in 1952, was equal to the combined power of all the bombs dropped on Germany and Japan in the Second World War - including the atomic ones.

15 May

Fred Astaire's first screen-test notes read: 'Can't act. Can't sing. Can dance a little.'

Only one Western film has ever been directed by a woman.

The first Academy Awards (or 'Oscars') were presented on 16 May 1929. The most successful person in the history of these awards is undoubtedly Walt Disney. Between 1931 and 1969 he collected thirty-five 'Oscars'.

The River Nile has been recorded as frozen over only twice – once in the ninth century, and then again in the eleventh century.

On average an acre of green land contains some fifty thousand spiders.

17 May

A manned rocket can reach the moon in less time than it used to take to travel the length of England by stagecoach.

18 May

Bertrand Russell, the English philosopher who was born today in 1872, was a prominent member of the original Campaign for Nuclear Disarmament. He was arrested and put in prison after a demonstration in 1961 at the age of eighty-nine, and was still actively campaigning for peace well into his nineties.

Someone suffering from coprolalia has an uncontrollable desire to be foul-mouthed.

19 May

In Ancient Greece, a woman's age was counted from the day of her marriage.

Eighty per cent of all body heat escapes through the head.

Sahara means 'desert' in Arabic.

20 May

Jesus was born in the reign of Herod, and it is known that Herod died in 4 BC. This means that Jesus was also born 'before Christ'. The mistake in dating was made in the sixth century, and has remained ever since.

It is illegal to drive a horse-drawn carriage in the City of London without a dispensation.

21 May

Until 1999, Neptune – not Pluto – is the planet farthest from the Sun.

The blood of a grasshopper is not red, but white.

22 May

The United States, which accounts for six per cent of the population of the world, consumes nearly sixty per cent of the world's resources.

Like most Elizabethan playwrights, Christopher Marlowe had his plays printed anonymously.

23 May

Pope Paul IV, who was elected on this day in 1555, was so outraged when he saw the naked bodies on the ceiling of the Sistine Chapel that he ordered Michelangelo to paint clothes on to them.

The Black Death claimed roughly forty million lives in the thirteenth century.

Golden toads are so rare that a biological reserve has been specially created for them.

24 May

Bob Dylan, the American musician, was born on 24 May 1941. When someone asked him what his songs were about, he replied: 'Some of them are about ten minutes long, others five or six.'

Cutting down a tree was a hanging offence in Britain until 1819.

In 1816, the poets Byron and Shelley, their friend Dr Polidori, and Shelley's wife Mary, all agreed to write a ghost story each while on holiday in Switzerland. It was the least famous of the quartet, Mary Shelley, who came up with the novel *Frankenstein*.

25 May

The temperature of the planet Mars can rise as high as eighty degrees Fahrenheit during the day, and sink as low as minus one-hundred-and-ninety degrees at night.

Thomas Crapper, a toilet salesman from London, wrote an autobiography entitled *Flushed With Pride*.

26 May

George Formby, the popular English singer who was born today in 1904, was awarded the Order of Lenin by Russia.

A pig was executed by public hanging in 1386 for the murder of a child.

You need to harvest an entire coffee tree for a year to produce just one pound of coffee.

27 May

It costs the West German Government over half a million pounds a year to keep the Nazi war criminal Rudolf Hess in Spandau Gaol.

The earliest recorded circumnavigation of the British Isles occurred in 325 BC, and was achieved by a Greek called Pytheas.

28 May

Fried mice were once used to cure smallpox in Britain.

You are not allowed to eat snakes on Sunday in Iraq.

There are about eight miles of roads on the main island of the Isles of Scilly, but only one petrol station.

29 May

Sir Edmund Hillary and Sherpa Tensing finally reached the summit of Mount Everest on 29 May 1953. They were helped on the climb by twelve other climbers, forty Sherpa guides, and over seven hundred porters.

After nuclear tests in the Sahara Desert, it was discovered that scorpions can withstand about two hundred times the amount of radiation which would kill a human being.

30 May

Joan of Arc was declared a witch and burnt at the stake on 30 May 1431. She eventually became Saint Joan in 1920.

Camel-hunting is illegal in Arizona.

31 May

Franz-Joseph Haydn, the composer who died on 31 May 1809, taught Beethoven harmony when the great man was still a student. However, like many others, he failed to recognise Beethoven's talent and advised him to give up music.

About one hundred people die every minute, but over two hundred are born.

There is only one whole number that can be added to itself, and multiplied with itself, and still produce the same result: two.

June

1 June

The Mormon leader, Brigham Young, who founded the religious centre in Salt Lake City in 1847, was born on 1 June 1801. The Mormon religion allows polygamy, and Brigham Young himself had at least twenty wives.

Burt Lancaster turned down the chance to play the lead in *Ben Hur*. The film went on to win eleven Oscars, including one for Lancaster's replacement, Charlton Heston.

2 June

Queen Elizabeth II was crowned on 2 June 1953. This particular day was chosen because meteorologists said it was the most consistently sunny day of the year. But it rained.

The British hangman, Albert Pierrepoint, once had the unpleasant task of putting to death a friend from his local pub.

A crow once built a nest made from barbed wire.

3 June

On 3 June 1956, a momentous historic event occurred which was destined to change the face of life in Britain – third-class railway travel was abolished.

A six-pound sea-hare can lay forty thousand eggs in a single minute.

At a steady walking pace you could walk all round the earth in exactly one year.

4 June

The Crown Jewels were kept in Aberystwyth during the Second World War.

In the eighteenth century, fashionable people wore false eyebrows made out of mouse-skin.

The number of children born in India each year (about twelve million) is equal to the entire population of Australia.

5 June

On 5 June 1783, the first hot-air balloon was invented. It was made of nothing stronger than paper.

In 1797, James Heatherington was fined £50 for wearing a top hat in public, after women had complained of being terrified by such a sight.

Many Oriental babies have a bruise mark on their bottoms until the age of two.

6 June

Shakespeare left no words of actual autobiography.

In 1978, the United Nations Food and Agricultural Organisation estimated that 'all the tea in China' amounted to 356 000 metric tons.

Yugoslavia has seven neighbouring countries which touch its borders – Italy, Austria, Hungary, Bulgaria, Romania, Albania, and Greece.

7 June

Eric the Red chose the name of Greenland for the icy country which he discovered in the tenth century, in order to encourage settlers.

The composer John Cage's piece *Imaginary Landscape No. 4* is scored for twelve radios tuned at random.

8 June

The mathematician Cardano was imprisoned for doing a horoscope of Jesus Christ.

In our galaxy, there are five billion stars bigger than the sun.

9 June

Charles Dickens, who died on this day in 1870, was an insomniac. He believed that he had the best chance of getting to sleep if he positioned himself exactly in the middle of the bed, which must at all times be pointing in a northerly direction.

The philosopher Descartes speculated that monkeys could in fact speak, but that they chose not to in order to avoid having to work.

10 June

The great American singer and actress Judy Garland was born today in 1922. Her original name was the distinctly unglamorous Frances Gumm.

In 1924, an eighteen-foot-high candle weighing three tons was erected in honour of the singer Enrico Caruso, in Naples.

The composer of the French revolutionary song, 'The Marseillaise', had once been a strong royalist.

11 June

The Formula One driver, Jackie Stewart, was born on this day in 1939. Not only has he won three motor-racing world championships, but he has also been British champion clay-pigeon shooter on no fewer than five occasions.

If the present birth-rate continues, New York will have a black majority by the end of the century.

The nineteenth-century US President Andrew Johnson was a slave as a child.

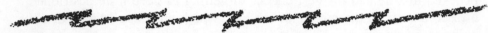

12 June

Thomas Arnold, who died on 12 June 1842, was headmaster of Rugby School at the time of the now famous 'handball' incident. During a game of football, a pupil decided to pick up the ball and run towards the opposition's line. This breach of the rules gave rise to the formation of a whole new game – Rugby.

Within a few years of Columbus' discovery of America, the Spaniards had killed one-and-a-half million Indians.

13 June

William Butler Yeats, who was born on 13 June 1865, is considered one of the greatest poets of the twentieth century. He wrote his most important poems between the age of fifty and seventy-five.

Two ordinary houseflies could produce 5 000 000 000 000 offspring in one season.

If the population of China walked past you in single file, the line would never end because of the rate of reproduction.

The inhabitants of Iceland are probably the most literate people in the world, reading more books per capita than any other country.

The Magna Carta was 'signed' on 15 June 1215 at Runnymede. King John didn't actually put his name to the document because he couldn't read or write, so he had to place his seal on it instead.

In 1562 a man was dug up six hours after his burial, after he had been seen to be breathing. He lived for another seventy-five years.

A scorpion could survive for three weeks if it was embedded in a block of ice.

16 June

Mary Stuart became Queen of Scotland at the tender age of six days.

Alexander the Great was tutored by the eminent Greek thinker Aristotle.

There are more nutrients in the cornflake packet itself than there are in the cornflakes.

17 June

June 17 was not only the date of birth of King John III of Poland but also the date of his coronation, his marriage, and ultimately his death.

The French painter Claude Monet won 100 000 francs in a state lottery, which enabled him to devote the rest of his life to painting.

Thomas Edison's sight improved in later life, but he still preferred to use Braille for his reading.

18 June

The battle of Waterloo was fought today in 1815, though the actual battlefield was some miles away from the British headquarters at Waterloo. In England, after the victory, 'Waterloo teeth' were sold as mementoes from the battle, having been ripped from the unfortunate French corpses.

The major export of Liechtenstein is false teeth.

Shoe sizes were once measured in barleycorns.

19 June

Queen Victoria inadvertently caused the death of her beloved Albert when the effluent pipe from her chamber burst, flooding his with dirty, disease-ridden water.

In 1908 the Moskva River in Russia rose nine metres, flooding 100 streets and 2500 houses.

If eighty per cent of your liver was removed, it could still function, and would eventually restore itself to its original size.

20 June

On 20 June 1756, 146 British men and women were locked in a small guardroom measuring fifteen feet by eighteen, in the Indian city of Calcutta. Only twenty-three people survived the ordeal, which became known as the 'Black Hole of Calcutta'.

There is about two hundred times more gold dissolved in the world's oceans than has been mined in our entire history.

21 June

Queen Berengaria, the wife of Richard I of England, never set foot on English soil.

The first edition of The Gospels to be written in the language of the Eskimos was printed in Copenhagen in 1744.

The founder of the Macdonald's hamburger chain is a Bachelor of Hamburgerology (BH).

22 June

On 22 June 1633, after threats of torture to himself and his family, Galileo was eventually forced to admit the falsehood of his theories of the universe. His accuser was none other than the Pope himself, who regarded the idea that the earth was not the centre of the universe as total blasphemy.

Not one new livestock animal has been domesticated in the last four thousand years.

23 June

On 23 June 1611, soon after he had discovered what later became known as Hudson River and Hudson Bay, the navigator Henry Hudson was cast adrift by his crew, and left to die. To this day no one knows exactly why the mutiny happened.

During the Second World War, the Americans had the idea of fitting bats with minature bombs which would then be dropped as they flew over the enemy.

Granada Television's long-running serial *Coronation Street* was originally entitled *Florizel Street*.

24 June

Lime (or calcium oxide), when heated, produces a brilliant white light, and used to be used to illuminate stages at the start of the century. Hence the phrase 'to be in the limelight'.

You use up more calories by eating a stick of celery than are contained in the stick itself.

25 June

Leonardo da Vinci invented an alarm clock which woke the sleeper by gently rubbing his feet.

The plant life contained in the oceans of the world makes up eighty-five per cent of the world's greenery.

26 June

When his wife Eleanor died, King Henry II had crosses built at every place that her body stopped on the journey to London for burial. The most famous is perhaps Charing Cross in London.

During the First World War, a sanitary policeman was placed outside each latrine to make sure the user convered up his excreta with earth.

The first time that a woman appeared on the stage completely nude was at the Folies-Bergère in Paris in 1912.

27 June

If you translate literally, the Chinese words 'kung fu' mean 'leisure time'.

There are as many rats in Britain as there are people.

Until the end of the eighteenth century, lions were used to guard the Tower of London.

The ball-point pen was invented by two brothers – George and Lazlo Biro.

28 June

The Indian atlas-moth has a twelve-inch wing span.

A kangaroo can only jump if its tail is touching the ground.

29 June

On average you lose eleven ounces a night while you are sleeping.

A female rhinoceros has to go through a pregnancy lasting 560 days.

Over a quarter of Russia is covered by forest.

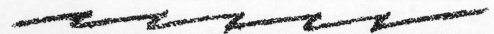

30 June

There are more germs in the human mouth than there are in the anus.

There is more pigment in brown eyes than there is in blue eyes.

Her Majesty's Stationery Office issues two million rolls of 'hard' toilet paper to the Civil Service and Armed Forces each year.

July

1 July

Nearly a quarter of all the bones in the human body can be found in the feet.

Sri Lanka is the second largest tea-producer in the world.

Soda water contains no soda.

Rhinoceros horn, which is much in demand, is not a horn at all, but is the animal's hair.

3 July

It was not until two years after his death that Oliver Cromwell was hanged and decapitated.

At a steady walking pace, it would take about twelve hours to walk off a pound of fat.

King Richard the Lionheart only spent five per cent of his reign in England.

4 July

Marie Curie, the Nobel Prize-winning scientist who discovered radium, suffered from her own discovery when, on 4 July 1934, she died as a result of over-exposure to radioactivity.

Crocodiles can see underwater because they have a semi-transparent third eyelid which slides into place when necessary.

Two-thirds of the body's weight is water.

5 July

In nearly every language in the world, the word for mother begins with an 'm' sound.

The 'funny bone' in our elbow is not a bone at all, but a nerve.

Costa Rica has no army.

6 July

William Shakespeare had eleven different ways of spelling his surname.

Between 1930 and 1934, there was no such thing as a speed limit in Britain.

Some of the canals in Venice have traffic lights.

7 July

Members of the House of Lords do not wear gloves in the presence of the Queen.

South Africa produces two-thirds of the world's gold.

Minus forty degrees centigrade is exactly the same as minus forty degrees Fahrenheit.

8 July

The most popular sport played in Britain is darts.

The volume of water in the Amazon is greater than the combined total of the next eight largest rivers in the world.

9 July

King Camp Gillette, the man who invented the first disposable safety razor, died on 9 July 1932. Two years after he first patented his invention he had only sold 168 blades, but by the following year sales had jumped to an incredible 12.4 million blades.

A father cannot be charged with infanticide.

Israeli women are the only women in the world who must undergo compulsory military service.

10 July

Lady Jane Grey became Queen of England on 10 July 1553 at the age of sixteen. She was queen for only nine days, before she was arrested and executed.

The Earth is the densest planet in our solar system.

Denmark has the oldest national flag in the world.

11 July

On 11 July 1962, Fred Baldsare became the first person to swim the English Channel underwater, using 'scuba' equipment.

If you're suffering from 'acute nasopharyngitis', you've got a cold.

A thick glass is more likely to crack than a thin one if you pour hot water into it.

12 July

The legs of a giraffe can break very easily.

Chief Sitting Bull was a medicine man, and did not join in the fighting at the Battle of the Little Big Horn.

13 July

On this day in 1798, William Wordsworth wrote his famous 'Lines composed a few miles above Tintern Abbey'. During his seven years as Poet Laureate later in his life, he wrote no poetry.

Baked beans were originally sold with treacle, not tomato sauce.

Nowhere in England is more than seventy-five miles from the sea.

14 July

A solar eclipse cannot last longer than seven minutes and fifty-eight seconds.

Shirley Temple was a dollar millionairess before the age of ten.

15 July

It is possible to extract aspirin from the bark of some trees.

The Red Sea is never mentioned in the Bible.

King Edward VIII is the only British monarch to have written an autobiography.

African witch-doctors only send their patients a bill if they expect them to live.

16 July

Hilaire Belloc, a writer of many talents, died on 16 July 1953. He had already written his own epitaph, which read: 'When I am dead, I hope it may be said: "His sins were scarlet, but his books were read."'

The people of Eire drink more tea per capita than any other country in the world.

The screwdriver was invented before the screw.

17 July

James Cagney was born on this day in 1899. Though he is most famous for his many gangster films, he started his career as a chorus girl, and his studio publicised the year of his birth as 1904 in order to capitalise on his baby face.

Only the male nightingale sings.

Most people blink about 15 000 times a day.

18 July

A chameleon's body is often only half the length of its tongue.

A tarantula, although it is a spider, cannot spin a web.

England is smaller than New England in America.

19 July

Georges Sand wrote all her novels at night.

Julius Caesar was an epileptic.

It was the custom for seventeenth-century English ladies to wear their wedding ring on their thumb.

20 July

The English Football Association Challenge Cup Competition was formed on 20 July 1871, to become better-known over the years as the FA Cup. The first final saw the 'Wanderers' beat the 'Royal Engineers' by one goal to nil, watched by a crowd of only two thousand.

If you fly from London to New York by Concorde, you can arrive at your destination two hours before the time of your departure.

The human body contains enough fat to produce seven bars of soap.

21 July

On 21 July 1969, bookmakers paid out £10000 to David Threlfall when Neil Armstrong became the first man to set foot on the moon. Mr Threlfall had bet £10 at 1000–1 in 1964 that a man would set foot on the moon within seven years.

A black widow spider can devour as many as twenty 'husbands' in a single day.

King George VI competed at the Wimbledon tennis championships.

22 July

There are 602 rooms in Buckingham Palace.

Nearly a quarter of the population of Poland was killed in the Second World War.

There are no rivers in Saudi Arabia.

23 July

Taiwan exports more mushrooms than any other country in the world.

Scientists have found that the number of UFO sightings increase when Mars is nearest the Earth.

24 July

The first man to swim the English Channel without a life-jacket was Captain Matthew Webb. He completed the crossing in August 1875 in 21 hours 45 minutes. He died eight years later on 24 July 1883, as he was attempting another record by swimming the rapids above the Niagara Falls.

An owl can turn its head in a complete circle.

The inspiration for Defoe's Robinson Crusoe was a sailor called Alexander Selkirk who spent four years alone on a desert island.

25 July

After a weekend at Sandringham, guests of Edward VII were weighed to see if they had eaten well.

Stalin, who was responsible for a great deal of religious persecution in Russia, studied theology as a young man.

Our own galaxy is minute compared to the radio galaxies being discovered at the edge of the universe.

26 July

The British novelist Aldous Huxley was born on 26 July 1894. An illness during childhood left his sight seriously impaired, but he did not give up his ambition to be a writer, and actually learnt Braille in order to keep up with his reading.

The human head is a quarter of our total length at birth, but only an eighth of our total length by the time we reach adulthood.

27 July

Vincent Van Gogh, who shot himself on this day in 1890 at the age of thirty-seven, was a painter whose greatness was only recognised after his tragic suicide. It is doubtful whether he sold more than one or two paintings in his whole lifetime.

At birth a panda weighs only four ounces, and is about the same size as a mouse.

28 July

One of the greatest natural disasters of recent centuries occurred on this day in 1976, when an earthquake hit Tangshan in China, killing three-quarters of a million people.

England's Stonehenge is 1500 years older than Rome's Colosseum.

29 July

The BBC put out the first televised weather forecast on 29 July 1949, though I have not been able to find out whether their prediction was right or wrong.

King George V was an avid stamp collector, and amassed over three hundred albums during his lifetime.

Dirty snow melts more quickly than clean snow.

30 July

Henry Ford, the famous car manufacturer who was born on 30 July 1863, subsidised an anti-Semitic newspaper and had a picture of Adolf Hitler on his desk.

In 1896, Britain and Zanzibar were at war for only thirty-eight minutes.

From fertilisation to birth, a baby's weight increases 5000 million times.

31 July

Both Elvis Presley and his mother died when they were the same age – forty-two.

Ninety per cent of Indian girls are married by the age of twenty.

August

1 August

Louis Blériot, the French aviator who died on 1 August 1936, was the first person to fly across the English Channel, in 1909. The journey, which took thirty-six-and-a-half minutes, ended with Blériot crash-landing his plane near Dover Castle.

Irving Berlin's 'White Christmas' has sold over one hundred million copies.

2 August

More coffee is consumed per capita in Sweden than in any other country.

Until 1879, any British soldier found guilty of bad conduct was reminded of his crime by having the initials 'BC' tattooed on his body.

The Battle of Hastings took place on King Harold's birthday.

3 August

On 3 August 1492, Christopher Columbus left Spain on his historic voyage to the New World. The expedition was run on a shoestring budget, and the total cost in terms of today's money would be just under £4000.

The first person to be buried in the famous Poet's Corner in Westminster Abbey was Geoffrey Chaucer.

The last dodo died in 1681.

India makes more films every year than any other country in the world.

4 August

Glaciers cover about ten per cent of the earth's surface.

The average height of a man in the Middle Ages was five feet six inches.

A caterpillar has three times as many muscles in its body as a human being.

5 August

Marilyn Monroe probably died after taking an overdose of sleeping pills on 5 August 1962. Her second husband, the baseball player Joe Dimaggio, has had fresh roses placed on her grave three times a week ever since.

Men are ten times more likely to be colour-blind than women.

Nearly fifty-five million people died as a result of the Second World War.

6 August

On 6 August 1945, an American B-29 bomber dropped the first atom bomb on the Japanese city of Hiroshima. One hundred thousand people died that day, and a similar number were killed by the resulting radiation.

If you are forced to pay out a ransom to a kidnapper in America you can at least take comfort from the fact that the money is tax-deductible.

Milk is heavier than cream.

7 August

Birds cannot fly much higher than 25 000 feet – which is about the height of Mount Everest.

Football was played in the twelfth century, though without any rules.

8 August

On 8 August 1963, the Glasgow-to-London mail train was robbed of over two-and-a-half million pounds. The incident became known as the Great Train Robbery, and though nearly all the men have now been caught, only £350 000 has been recovered.

All the New Testament writers were Jewish except St Luke.

9 August

Ice-hockey pucks travel at speeds of up to one hundred miles an hour.

You cannot be excommunicated from the Hindu religion.

One hundred and twenty drops of water are needed to fill a teaspoon.

10 August

Otto Lilienthal, the pioneering German aviator, died on 10 August 1896. He was killed after his glider crashed.

Hungary exports more hippopotamuses than any other country in Europe.

11 August

In the early days of the colony of Virginia, you could be executed for damaging or attempting to damage a tobacco plant.

Flamingoes have to hold their heads upside-down to eat.

Giraffes show their affection for each other by rubbing necks.

12 August

The Ancient Greeks believed that boys developed in the right-hand side of the womb, and girls in the left.

The legs of Disraeli's bed were placed in bowls of salty water to ward off evil spirits.

Twice as many men as women commit suicide.

13 August

Queen bees can lay three thousand eggs in just one day.

There is only one inanimate sign of the Zodiac – Libra.

14 August

On 14 August 1908, the first international beauty contest in Britain was held at the Pier Hippodrome in Folkestone, Kent.

We put only five per cent of the earth's plant life to any practical use.

The frankfurter originated in China.

15 August

The French town of Bayonne gave its name to the bayonet.

The official name for Libya is the Socialist People's Libyan Arab Jamahiriya.

Milan cathedral took nearly six hundred years to build.

Iraq supplies three-quarters of the world's dates.

16 August

There are six million trees in The Forest of Martyrs near Jerusalem, symbolising the Jewish death toll in the Second World War.

Rubber is an important ingredient in the manufacture of bubble-gum.

In Wales, sheep outnumber people by nearly two to one.

17 August

The Incas and the Aztecs led a perfectly 'civilised' life without the wheel.

There are no 'roads', only 'streets', in the City of London.

Human adults breathe about 23 000 times a day.

18 August

There is enough petrol in a full tank of a jumbo jet to drive an average car four times round the world.

The door to 10 Downing Street, home of Britain's Prime Minister, opens only from the inside.

Seventy-five per cent of the inhabitants of Norway live within ten miles of the sea.

19 August

Every continent in the world contains a city called Rome.

Half the world exists on a basic diet of rice.

Most mammals are colour-blind.

20 August

Snow has fallen on London on Christmas Day only seven times since the start of the century.

The word 'girl' appears only once in the Bible.

The American poet Emily Dickinson used to talk to visitors from an adjoining room, because she was so self-conscious about her appearance.

21 August

Oliver Cromwell's real name was Oliver Williams.

The Chinese wear white at funerals.

There is a gypsy convention every year at Saintes-Maries-de-la-Mer in France.

The Bank of England has its own independent water supply.

22 August

The American writer Dorothy Parker was born on this day in 1893. In 1950 she remarried her husband, Alan Campbell, after they had been divorced for three years. When someone at the reception remarked that some of the guests hadn't spoken to one another for years, Parker immediately quipped, 'Including the bride and groom'.

There is a delicatessen for dogs in New York.

There is an underpass across the M5 motorway near Exeter which was built for the exclusive use of badgers.

23 August

Rudolph Valentino died from a perforated ulcer on 23 August 1926. Thousands of women lined his funeral route, and there was rioting as the coffin was carried past.

The word 'school' comes from an old Greek word meaning 'leisure'.

An Alsatian's sense of smell is a million times better than a human's.

24 August

When people first started sending letters in Britain, it was the recipient who paid the postage.

Turtles have no teeth.

It takes sixty seconds for blood to make one complete circuit of the human body.

25 August

Sean Connery, the actor who played James Bond for many years, was born today in 1930. Before he made his fortune in the film business he had a variety of jobs, including one as a coffin-polisher.

The idea of Santa Claus as a fat, old man with white hair and whiskers, dressed in a red suit, was invented by a nineteenth-century American artist.

26 August

It is the larvae of moths which damage clothes, not the moths themselves.

The first victim of the electric chair took eight minutes to die.

27 August

The chemist who discovered barbituric acid named it after his wife, Barbara.

Typewriters were originally conceived as an aid to the blind.

Figures show that the most popular time for dying in the United States is in the first two months of the year.

28 August

Over twenty million Africans were transported to America and the Caribbean during the three hundred years of the slave trade.

Hammerfest in Norway is the most northerly town in the world.

The old X-certificate rating for films was introduced to Britain in 1951.

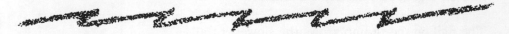

29 August

The Swedish actress Ingrid Bergman was born on 29 August 1915, and died on the same day in 1982. She caused a major scandal in Hollywood in 1951 when she gave birth to a child by the married Italian film director, Roberto Rossellini, and it took several years before she was forgiven by the American public.

Half of all the different types of flowers in the world can be found in South America.

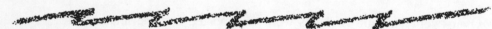

30 August

King Louis XI of France died on this day in 1483. He once commanded one of his abbots to invent a new and ridiculous musical instrument for the amusement of the Court. The Abbot gathered together a series of pigs, each with their own distinctive squeal, and proceeded to prick each of them in turn to provide the desired tune.

The world's first parking meters were installed in Oklahoma in 1935.

31 August

The Roman Emperor Caligula, whose nickname was 'Little Boots', was born on 31 August, AD 12. At the age of twenty-five he decided to make himself a god, and his horse a senator.

The nail on the thumb grows the slowest of all.

The most common disease in the world is tooth decay.

September

1 September

Pope Adrian IV died on 1 September 1159. His real name was Nicholas Breakspear, and he is the only Englishman ever to become the head of the Roman Catholic Church.

Ice-cream was invented in 1620.

Snakes have their hearing equipment in their jaws.

2 September

On this day in 1666, the Great Fire of London began at the bakery of Thomas Farriner in Pudding Lane. Though an enormous amount of property was burnt, only six people were killed.

The Japanese Santa Claus is a woman.

The average man will spend about 145 days of his life shaving.

Mozart wrote the music for the song 'Twinkle Twinkle, Little Star' when he was only five years old.

3 September

The film actor Alan Ladd was born on 3 September 1913. Though only five feet six inches tall, he made his name playing tough guys, and was the first to speak the immortal line: 'A man's gotta do what a man's gotta do.'

George Washington was the first person to wear false teeth.

There are no telephones in Greenland.

Marco Polo brought spaghetti back from China.

4 September

The breed of dog we call the Great Dane originated in Germany, not Denmark.

The first letter of Christ's name in Greek is 'X' – hence the abbreviation 'Xmas'.

Robert Louis Stevenson wrote *Travels on a Donkey* during his honeymoon.

5 September

The human stomach can only hold about five pints of liquid.

Camels' humps do not contain water, they contain fat.

Rice paper is not made from rice.

6 September

Most people change their sleeping position at least twenty times a night.

Turkish baths were invented by the Romans.

The Chinese were the first people to use wallpaper.

The Pont Neuf (New Bridge) in Paris is not new at all. In fact, it is one of the oldest bridges in the city.

7 September

On this day in 1892, 'Gentleman' Jim Corbett beat J. L. Sullivan in twenty-one rounds to become the first world heavyweight boxing champion under the new Queensbury rules. They stipulated that gloves had to be worn, and that each round should last exactly three minutes.

Haggis was invented by the Ancient Greeks.

The Virgin Mary is the subject of twice as many biographies as Jesus.

8 September

There is a town in West Virginia, USA, called Looneyville.

The novel *Les Miserables* by Victor Hugo contains the longest sentence ever published. It is 823 words long.

9 September

When William the Conqueror died on 9 September 1087, he was buried at Rouen in France. In 1562, vandals broke into his tomb and stole everything but his thighbone, but during the French revolution, that too was taken.

Cleopatra's Needle, the obelisk situated on the Victoria Embankment in London, was built over fourteen centuries before the birth of Cleopatra.

10 September

On 10 September 1897, a taxi-driver called George Smith became the first motorist in England to be convicted for drunken driving.

The fifty-two cards in a normal pack are meant to symbolise the number of weeks in a year.

The game of marbles was introduced to Britain by the Romans.

11 September

The prison on the Isle of Sark has room for only two people.

Gorillas cannot swim.

Battersea Dogs' Home has to deal with about 15 000 stray dogs every year.

Verdi's opera *Aida*, was written to commemorate the opening of the Suez Canal.

12 September

The first policewoman ever was appointed on 12 September 1910 in America. She was Alice Wells of the Los Angeles Police Department.

Sunglasses were originally worn by Hollywood film stars not to look 'cool', but to protect their eyes against the harsh studio lights.

13 September

The French film actress Claudette Colbert was born on 13 September 1905. She won an Academy Award for her role opposite Clark Gable in the 1934 film *It Happened One Night*. It was the first movie to win all four major awards – Best Actor, Best Actress, Best Director, and Best Film – a distinction it shares with only one other film, *One Flew over the Cuckoo's Nest*.

King Constantine of Greece won an Olympic gold medal for sailing.

14 September

The Duke of Wellington died on this day in 1852. At his funeral in St Paul's Cathedral, there were seven thousand gas lamps placed all around the church to light up the procession.

In medical language, a moron is more intelligent than an idiot.

Submarines were invented in the early seventeenth century.

15 September

An ant can pull a load three times its own weight.

Uranus was originally named *Georgium Sidium* after George III of England.

America did not have a national anthem until 1931.

16 September

Albert Einstein failed his university entrance exams at his first attempt.

In 1945 some starlings perched on the second hand of Big Ben in London, causing it to lose five minutes.

Your hair stands on end just before you are struck by lightning.

17 September

Napoleon travelled in a bullet-proof coach.

Alcohol does not warm you up, but actually causes your body-temperature to drop.

Fifty per cent of the world's population live in under five per cent of the total land area.

18 September

The film actress Greta Garbo, who was christened Greta Gustafsson, was born on 18 September 1905. She made her screen debut at the age of sixteen in an advertising film called *How Not to Wear Clothes*.

The Chinese eat a soup made from birds' nests.

19 September

On 19 September 1893, New Zealand became the first country in the world to give women the right to vote. The United States followed twenty-seven years later.

The right side of the human brain controls the left side of the body and vice versa.

Gorillas do not eat meat.

Ninety per cent of all fires are man-made.

20 September

Jacob Grimm died on this day in 1863. He is most famous for the book of fairy tales he collected with his brother Wilhelm, but he also started the important *German Dictionary* in 1852. It was finally completed by other scholars in 1960.

Canada's coastline is six times longer than that of Australia.

There are no bones in an elephant's trunk, just 40 000 muscles.

21 September

The peacock is the symbol of resurrection in many pieces of early Christian art.

A normal spider has about six hundred silk glands on its body which it uses to spin its web.

The Italians used to block the tops of their wine bottles with oil before they thought of using cork.

22 September

On 22 September 1955, Britain's first commercial television channel began broadcasting. The first advert was for Gibbs SR toothpaste.

Bikinis were named after the Bikini Atoll in the Pacific, where the Americans carried out a series of atomic bomb tests.

The River Thames froze over in the winter of 1890–91.

23 September

Scotland exports sand to Saudi Arabia.

Big Ben in London is not the name of the clock, but the bell inside it.

Cats spend well over half of their lives asleep.

24 September

The American writer F. Scott Fitzgerald was born on 24 September 1896. For most of his life he suffered from an excess of insulin which resulted in a low blood-sugar level. To compensate for this, Fitzgerald used to drink heavily-sweetened coffee, and he had a craving for Coca-Cola and fudge.

The 'white' statues of Ancient Rome and Greece were originally painted in bright colours.

Cucumbers are fruits, not vegetables.

25 September

On 25 September 1978, Mary Fuller of California had a human body come crashing through her car windscreen. It had been thrown from a plane crash nearby.

The dog Rin Tin Tin was voted the most popular film performer of the year in 1926.

One of the most efficient ways of cleaning your teeth is to chew on a stick.

Horses can sleep standing up.

26 September

There is a red star called *Epsilon Aurigae* which is 27 000 million times bigger than our Sun.

Some British zoos have had to put their lionesses on the pill to prevent unwanted pregnancies.

27 September

Canada has more lakes than the rest of the world put together.

Though Switzerland is a neutral country, it has compulsory military service.

28 September

On 28 September 1894, Marks and Spencer opened their first shop – a penny bazaar in Manchester. They have, of course, expanded since then, and now over sixty per cent of all women in Britain buy their underwear from branches of Marks and Spencer all over the country.

White ants are not ants; they are termites.

The manufacturers of 'Monopoly' print more 'money' each year than the United States Treasury.

Admiral Nelson never fully got over his seasickness.

The female ants are the ones who do all the work.

Even fairly well-educated people use only one per cent of the possible words in the English language when talking to each other.

30 September

Gale warnings were first issued in 1861.

It is estimated that there are nearly half a million sauna baths in Finland.

October

1 October

The English actress Julie Andrews was born on 1 October 1935. After the phenomenal success of *The Sound of Music* and *Mary Poppins*, she became typecast as the sweet English rose, and in 1966 she was quoted as saying: 'I don't want to be thought of as wholesome.'

Honey-bees die after they deliver their first sting.

A real diamond should be cold to the touch.

2 October

Though the normal year has 365 days, the lunar year has only 364.

White bread was originally used only in church services.

The French call the Battle of Waterloo the Battle of Mont St Jean.

3 October

As long ago as 3 October 1811, a county cricket match was played between the women of Hampshire and the women of Surrey.

There is a city in the Sahara which is built entirely of salt.

There is only one lake in Scotland; the other areas of inland water are called lochs.

4 October

The American rock singer Janis Joplin died on 4 October 1970. She left $2500 in her will 'so that my friends can get blasted after I'm gone'.

During the Second World War a Japanese sergeant went to hide in the jungles of Guam. He only came out to surrender twenty-eight years after the end of the war.

What we call a 'black eye' is called a 'blue eye' in German.

5 October

The English champion jockey Gordon Richards rode his twelfth consecutive winner in three days on 5 October 1933. He rode eleven of them at Chepstow Racecourse, following the initial winner at Nottingham.

Ships can travel faster in cold water than in warm.

Eggs are sold on bits of string in Korea.

6 October

On 6 October 1850, Alfred, Lord Tennyson died. Both Tennyson and his predecessor, William Wordsworth wore exactly the same suit to the ceremony which marked their inauguration as Poet Laureate. And both borrowed it off another man, Samuel Rogers.

The largest meat-eating land-animal in Britain is the badger.

7 October

The American who invented a revolutionary process for deep-freezing food died on 7 October 1956. His name was Clarence Birdseye.

Cars were first started with ignition keys in 1949.

The first gramophone record consisted of only five words – 'Mary had a little lamb'.

8 October

On 8 October 1976, a light aeroplane flew over the Piazza Venezia in Rome and dropped hundreds of bank notes on to the heads of unsuspecting passers-by. The mysterious pilot was never found.

The practice of numbering houses only began in 1764.

A normal swarm of locusts would consist of at least one million insects.

9 October

The singer-songwriter John Lennon was born on 9 October 1940 during an air raid. He was given the patriotic middle name of Winston.

Moths have neither mouths nor stomachs.

The cashew-nut belongs to the same family as poison ivy.

10 October

The Italian composer Giuseppe Verdi was born on 10 October 1813. His operas were hugely successful during his lifetime, and many contained a powerful political message.

The first woman to take a seat in the British House of Commons, Lady Astor, was born in America.

Solar energy was used as a source of power in the seventeenth century.

11 October

The food manufacturer, H. J. Heinz, was born today in 1844. He will go down in history as the 'inventor' of baked beans, well over eight million tins of which are sold each year.

Lobsters have blue blood.

William Shakespeare was the first person to use the word 'lonely'.

12 October

An ordinary English nurse called Edith Cavell helped over two hundred Allied soldiers to escape from German-occupied Belgium during the First World War. She was executed by firing squad on 12 October 1915.

Dogs' teeth were used as a form of currency in the Solomon Islands until recently.

The glass cat-fish is almost totally transparent.

13 October

There are over three times as many countries north of the equator as there are south of it.

Queen Ranavalona of Madagascar decreed that if any of her subjects appeared in her dreams, they would be killed.

A pound of lemons contains more sugar than a pound of strawberries.

14 October

Dwight D. Eisenhower was born on 14 October 1890. He was to become the first five-star general in American history, and in 1944 he helped plan the Allied invasion of Europe. The parents of this great military figure were members of a fundamentalist religious organisation called the River Brethren Sect, which openly advocates pacifism.

Red Indians used to smoke through their noses.

15 October

Venus is the only planet in our solar system which rotates in a clockwise direction.

The oldest museum in the world is the Ashmolean in Oxford.

Under one per cent of the islands in the Caribbean are inhabited.

16 October

Bombay duck is made from dried fish.

Windsor Castle, the country residence of the British Royal Family, is the largest castle in the world that is still inhabited.

Nine-tenths of the Vitamin C present in Brussels sprouts is lost when they are cooked.

17 October

The American stunt-rider Evel Knievel was born on 17 October 1938. He is known for his daredevil motorbike jumps, and has broken over 100 bones in his lifetime. He now claims that he is so used to being operated on that he doesn't even need a proper anaesthetic.

Christopher Columbus's crew on his voyage to the New World consisted of about one hundred convicts.

18 October

The word 'Amen' is used not only by Christians, but by Jews and Moslems as well.

The most common first name in the world is Mohammed.

The Arabian Gulf States of Qatar, Bahrain, and Kuwait – three of the richest countries in the world – do not charge income tax.

19 October

The 'King of Bells' in the Kremlin was cast on 19 October 1773. It is over twenty feet high and weighs nearly two hundred tons, but it has never been rung as it cracked on being released from the mould.

20 October

The English swallow takes about thirty days to migrate to Africa.

More perfume is used in Russia than in any other country in the world.

Silkworms are not worms but caterpillars.

You cannot transmit a radio signal from a submerged submarine to land.

21 October

On 21 October 1966, disaster struck the small Welsh mining village of Aberfan. A colliery slag tip slid down the side of a hill and engulfed a row of houses, a farm, and a school. Of the 144 people who died, 116 were children.

Jack the Ripper was left-handed.

Several models of an ape were used for the 1933 film *King Kong*: the smallest was only eighteen inches tall.

22 October

On 22 October 1797, the first parachute jump in history was made over Parc Monceau in Paris by Andre Garnerin. He did not jump from an aeroplane, but from a balloon.

Every day, seven-and-a-half million tons of water evaporate from the Dead sea.

More people are killed each year by bees than by poisonous snakes.

23 October

The Battle of El-Alamein began on 23 October 1942. Fewer British soldiers died in this week-long battle than died in the Battle of Oudenarde in 1708, which lasted just one day.

If you lived on the planet Mercury, you would have four birthdays in a single Earth year.

John Wayne's real name was Marion Morrison.

24 October

The Norwegian diplomat Vidkun Quisling was born on 24 October 1887. During the Second World War he became a Nazi collaborator, and was executed by firing squad in 1945. His name has gone down in history as the one given to all traitors.

There is a type of cow called a 'Why'.

April Fool's Day is referred to as Boob Day in Spain.

25 October

Two of the most famous battles in British history were fought on this day. In 1414, Henry V scored his famous victory at Agincourt. In 1854, at Balaclava, the Charge of the Light Brigade was begun by Lord Cardigan: there were very heavy losses.

The most common name for a public house in Britain is 'The Red Lion'.

26 October

The Siberian larch accounts for one-fifth of the world's trees.

The stripes of a zebra are white, not black.

In America, a man called Al Cohol was once charged with being drunk.

Shooting-stars are not stars, but burning meteors.

27 October

The Welsh poet Dylan Thomas was born on this day in 1914. He is most famous for his poetry, but he also wrote the radio play *Under Milk Wood*. The action is set in a fictional Welsh village called Llareggub, which spells 'Buggerall' backwards.

Only human beings sleep on their backs.

The Red Sea is not red, it's blue.

28 October

The Statue of Liberty was officially dedicated on 28 October 1886. It was a present from the French Government to mark the one-hundredth anniversary of the Declaration of Independence, and was designed by Gustave Eiffel.

Pepsi-Cola was originally designed as a hangover cure.

More people live in Asia than in all other continents put together.

29 October

Sir Walter Raleigh was executed on 29 October 1618. It is widely thought that he introduced tobacco to Europe, but the distinction should be accorded to someone else – a Frenchman call Jean Nicot.

To type the word 'typewriter', you only have to use the top row of letter keys.

30 October

On 30 October 1938, Orson Welles produced a radio version of H. G. Wells' *The War of The Worlds*. The programme, which dealt with a fictional Martian invasion of the world, caused panic throughout America despite constant assurances that it was not real 'news'.

Lord Byron's last word was: 'Goodnight'.

The average iceberg weighs twenty million tons.

31 October

The famous escapologist Harry Houdini died on this day in 1926. For a man who performed so many stunts, it is ironic that he should have been killed by a simple blow to the stomach, at a moment when the great man was unprepared.

The first breakfast cereal to be produced was Shredded Wheat.

November

1 November

On this day in 1755, Lisbon in Portugal suffered one of the most powerful earthquakes ever recorded. Although it happened before machines had been invented to measure such phenomena, experts believe it may have had a magnitude of as much as 9. The biggest measured earthquake in modern times had a magnitude of 8.9.

The French painter Paul Gauguin helped in the construction of the Panama Canal.

More people in the world drink goats' milk than cows' milk.

2 November

Today, in 1924, the first crossword appeared in Britain. It was published in the *Sunday Express*.

All sweet things are tasted at the tip of the tongue only.

A rat can last longer without water than a camel.

3 November

On 3 November 1903, the small country of Panama became independent. The Panama hat, supposedly one of its most famous exports, in fact originates from Ecuador.

Queen Elizabeth I became totally bald in later life.

One of the original ingredients in Coca-Cola was the drug cocaine.

4 November

On this day in 1963, the Beatles played at the Royal Variety Performance in front of a distinguished audience. John Lennon introduced a song with the words 'Those in the cheaper seats clap. The rest of you, rattle your jewellery'.

The animal with the biggest brain in relation to its body is the ant.

Peanuts are used in the production of dynamite.

5 November

The fifth of November is celebrated as Guy Fawkes' Day, in remembrance of an unsuccessful attempt to blow up the Houses of Parliament in 1605. During the eighteenth century it was actually illegal not to celebrate this day. The law was eventually repealed in 1859.

One of the most famous statues in the world, *The Thinker* by Rodin, is actually a portrait of the Italian poet, Dante.

6 November

Scientists insist that everybody dreams – it's just that some people don't remember their dreams.

The least-used letter in the English language is the letter 'Q'.

Crocodiles cannot move their tongues because they are firmly attached to the roof of their mouths.

7 November

The Evangelist Billy Graham was born today in 1918. Nicknamed 'The Preaching Windmill', he once claimed that Heaven is exactly 1600 miles above the Earth.

Sharks are totally immune to cancer.

The human brain is about eighty per cent water.

8 November

Bram Stoker, the man who wrote the horror classic *Dracula,* was born today in 1847. It was actually a part of English law until 1824 to drive a wooden stake through the heart of any suicide victim to prevent them from turning into a vampire.

Ninety-seven per cent of the world's water is to be found in the oceans.

9 November

American actress Katherine Hepburn was born today in 1909. Her success record at the annual Academy Awards is phenomenal. She has been nominated thirteen times, and has won the Oscar for Best Actress four times.

The Sahara Desert is about the same size as the whole of Europe.

10 November

The actor Richard Burton was born today in 1925. Undoubtedly a great actor, he was perhaps most famous for his stormy relationship with Elizabeth Taylor. He showered her with presents during their two marriages, including a £500 000 diamond and a £60 000 mink coat.

The modern bra was invented after women athletes at the 1928 Olympics complained that such competitive running often resulted in severe bruising.

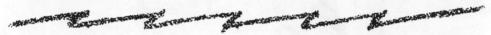

11 November

American soldier General Patton was born on 11 November 1885. He believed that he had had six previous lives, including a spell in the army of Alexander the Great, and a period as a prehistoric warrior.

The colour of mourning at funerals in Turkey is violet.

The shortest verse in The Bible is 'Jesus wept.'

12 November

On this day in 1956, the largest iceberg in the world was discovered in the South Pacific Ocean. It was bigger than Belgium.

More herrings are eaten worldwide than any other fish.

George Washington often carried a sundial around with him to tell the time, rather than a watch.

13 November

The writer R. L. Stevenson was born today in 1859. He claimed that his famous story *The Strange Case of Dr Jekyll and Mr Hyde* appeared to him in its totality in a dream one night.

Only female bees do any work for the hive.

The banana cannot reproduce itself without human help.

14 November

On 14 November 1973, Princess Anne and Captain Mark Phillips were married in London. At the Wolverhampton Races that day, the two-thirty 'Wedding Stakes' was won by a horse called 'Royal Mark'.

Some Chinese typewriters have over five thousand different characters.

15 November

The last of the Manchu Emperors, Pu Yi, came to power today in 1908, aged just two-and-a-half years. After the takeover of Mao Tse-Tung and the Communist Party, he ended up as an odd-job-man at the Botanical Gardens in Peking.

Your nose continues to grow throughout your life.

The word 'love', as used in tennis to mean 'no score', comes from the French word 'L'oeuf', meaning 'egg'. An egg was presumably thought to be shaped like a zero.

16 November

Probably the greatest meteor shower of all time occurred on this night in 1966, in the skies above the northern part of the Pacific Ocean. At one point more than two thousand meteors a minute passed overhead.

Everyone's tongue print is different.

Natural gas has no smell. An odour is added to prevent people ignoring dangerous gas leaks.

17 November

On this day in 1913, the first ship sailed through the newly-completed Panama Canal. Amid the celebrations, there was also cause for great sorrow. Over twenty-five thousand lives were lost during the construction of the Canal.

The original name given to the butterfly was the 'flutterby'.

Only humans cry.

18 November

There are only two words in the English language which include all the vowels, and in the correct order – 'facetious' and 'abstemious'.

There are more Irish in New York than in the whole of Dublin.

The male praying mantis can continue copulating with the female even after she has started eating him.

19 November

Abraham Lincoln made a famous speech on this day in 1863, after the crucial Battle of Gettysburg. It finished with the now-legendary promise of 'Government of the people, by the people, for the people'.

In Iceland, the telephone directories list people according to their first names.

20 November

Queen Elizabeth and Prince Philip married in Westminster Abbey on this day in 1947. Among their wedding presents were a racehorse from the Aga Khan, and a hand-made piece of lace from Mahatma Gandhi.

During the American Civil War, maggots were used to eat away the dead tissue around wounds.

21 November

The skull of the ancient Piltdown man was discovered by Charles Dawson on this day in 1912. Even though many scientists were convinced of its importance, the discovery was eventually declared a hoax, and caused one of the greatest scandals of the day.

Eleanor of Aquitaine was married to both the King of France and the King of England.

22 November

On 22 November 1963, millions of people all over the world witnessed the assassination of President John F. Kennedy. Amazingly, at the time, it was not a felony under US Federal Law to kill the President.

In terms of physical effort, a watch-repairer probably uses twice as much energy dressing in the morning as he does in his normal working hours.

23 November

Harpo Marx, the frizzy-haired Marx Brother with the dirty raincoat, was born today in 1893. Although he acted the mute on film, Harpo could in fact speak quite normally.

The only animal with four knees is the elephant.

At least one million people a year in Asia and Africa die after being bitten by the malarial mosquito.

24 November

Charles Darwin's *The Origin of Species*, one of the most important books on evolution, was published today in 1859. The phrase, 'The survival of the fittest', was not thought-up by Darwin, however, but borrowed from another scientist, Herbert Spencer.

Indian ink comes from China.

Only ten words make up twenty per cent of everything we say.

25 November

The Mousetrap by Agatha Christie opened in London on 25 November 1952. It is still the longest-running show in the world.

Croissants were originally invented not in France, but in Austria.

The sea snake is a hundred times more venomous than any snake to be found on dry land.

26 November

Today in 1764, a 'great storm' raged over the whole of England. Terrible damage was caused, and over eight thousand people are thought to have lost their lives.

The proportion of right-handed to left-handed people in the world is reckoned to be about five to one.

27 November

On 27 November 1582, William Shakespeare married Anne Hathaway. The great writer was only eighteen years of age at the time.

The most prescribed drug in the United Kingdom is Valium.

28 November

Instant coffee is not new: it has been in use since the middle of the eighteenth century.

The Amazon River basin, with all its plant life, provides the world with about forty per cent of its oxygen.

Blond beards grow faster than dark ones.

29 November

The first of the five senses to deteriorate as you grow older is the sense of smell.

Lead pencils are not made of lead at all, but of graphite.

30 November

Sir Winston Churchill was born today in 1874. He was not always a success in life. In fact, he was bottom of the class for much of his time at Harrow, and only managed to get into the Sandhurst Military Academy on his third attempt.

King Louis XIV apparently had only three baths in his entire life.

December

1 December

Woody Allen, the American film-maker and comedian, was born today in 1935. His tragi-comic wit produced the phrase of being 'at two with nature'.

Most astronauts grow an inch or two during their period in space.

Two different alphabets are used in Yugoslavia.

2 December

The Marquis de Sade, the man who gave his name to sadism, died on this day in 1814. His books are still officially banned in France.

More than half the babies born every day arrive before breakfast.

The chaffinch cannot sing anything original, it can only imitate the songs of other birds.

3 December

On 3 December 1926, Agatha Christie disappeared after hearing her husband would continue his love affair with another woman. Ten days later she was found living in a health spa in Yorkshire. No explanation was given for her behaviour, though speculation ranged from amnesia to attempted suicide. The police-search for Agatha Christie was exhaustive, and was reputed to have included over fifteen thousand volunteers.

Piranha fish can strip a horse of all its flesh in under a minute.

There are about seven million lamp-posts in Britain.

4 December

On 4 December 1952, a freak weather change saw the City of London enveloped by a layer of deadly smog, which literally left people gasping for breath. After five days, the death toll came to over four thousand, and thousands more died later from related illnesses.

Elizabeth I had over eighty wigs to choose from.

5 December

Walt Disney, who was born today in 1901, went bankrupt early on in his life. His company, Laugh-O-Gram-Corp, collapsed in 1923, but the young Walt soon recovered and went on to become one of the richest men in America.

People are on average a quarter of an inch taller at night than they are during the day.

The oldest fish on record is a sturgeon.

6 December

The average life-span in Ancient Rome was twenty-two years.

About one-sixth of the population of Britain eats custard at least once a day.

Each day about ten million people celebrate the same birthday.

7 December

Probably the longest unbroken peace between major nations is that between England and Portugal. They have never been at war with each other.

George I of England could neither speak nor write English.

If you cut a starfish up into chunks, each piece has the ability to grow into a whole new starfish.

Seventeen per cent of the world's caviar is consumed on the *QE2* every year.

8 December

Bulls can run faster uphill than downhill.

Over four hundred films have been made of the plays of William Shakespeare.

9 December

On this day in 1916, Issur Danielovitch Demsky was born. That was his real name – his stage name was Kirk Douglas.

There are over one-hundred-million light-sensitive cells in the retina of the human eye.

The eastern slope of Mont Blanc is in Italy; the summit is in France.

10 December

Alfred Nobel died on 10 December 1896. The major invention of his life was dynamite, but he is more likely to be remembered as the instigator of the world-famous Nobel Prize.

In every country in the world, the life-span of women is noticeably longer than that of men.

11 December

Edward VIII, Duke of Windsor, announced his abdication at 10 p.m. on this day in 1936. He is the only English king never to be crowned.

Seals can dive to depths of one thousand feet.

The scientific term for fear of beards is pogonophobia.

12 December

The inventor of the hovercraft, Sir Christopher Cockerell, finally got his idea patented on 12 December 1955. The first hovercraft public service came into being some six years later, when a twenty-four-passenger vehicle ran across the River Dee in England.

The music-hall entertainer Nosmo King invented his stage-name while looking at a 'No Smoking' sign.

13 December

Samuel Johnson, the man who wrote the first important English dictionary, died today in 1784. He once said to his biographer, Boswell, 'It matters not how a man dies, but how he lives.'

The Channel between England and France widens by about a foot every year.

14 December

King George VI was born today in 1895. His Christian name was in fact Albert, but he rejected it in favour of George to respect Queen Victoria's wish that no future British king should bear her husband's name.

One hundred thousand small toads once fell out of the air and landed on a village in France.

Pigeons were the main source of fresh meat for the people of the Middle Ages.

15 December

Sitting Bull, the Red Indian Chief of the Sioux tribes, died on this day in 1890. His bones were originally laid to rest in North Dakota, but businessmen from his native South Dakota wanted to have him moved to a more natural resting place. When their campaign was rejected, they stole the bones, and they now reside in Sitting Bull Park, South Dakota.

When she was seventy years old, the actress Sarah Bernhardt played the part of the teenage Juliet in Shakespeare's *Romeo and Juliet*.

16 December

Karate, often regarded as Japan's national sport, did not come to that country until 1916.

Barnacles stay fastened to the same object for the whole of their lives.

Lightning strikes the earth about a hundred times every second.

The mullet fish only turns totally red after its death.

17 December

The Wright brothers managed the first power-driven flight by an aeroplane on this day in 1903. The distance covered by their historic flying machine was less than the length of the modern jumbo jet.

No two snowflakes have yet been discovered with the same crystal pattern.

You weigh slightly less when the moon is directly overhead, because of the pull of its gravity.

18 December

On 18 December 1865, slavery was finally abolished in the United States. On the same day in 1917, the US Congress introduced the prohibition of alcohol to the state governments.

Clouds gather at a greater height during the day than they do at night.

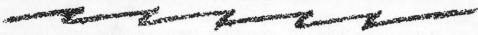

19 December

The English painter Joseph Turner died on this day in 1851. He was a gifted child, and his father, who was a barber, used to sell his twelve-year-old son's drawings to amazed customers.

Every time you step forward, you use fifty-four muscles.

Dogs are colour-blind.

20 December

The tallest member of Parliament in Britain was six feet six inches tall.

Coffins which are due for cremation are usually made with plastic handles.

The orang-utan's warning signal to would-be aggressors is a loud belch.

21 December

The Tory Prime Minister, Benjamin Disraeli, was born today in 1804. When asked what the difference between a calamity and a misfortune was, Disraeli replied, 'If Gladstone fell into the Thames it would be a misfortune, but if someone pulled him out again, it would be a calamity.'

Elephants sleep for only about two hours a day.

22 December

In relation to its size, the ordinary house-spider is as much as eight times faster than an Olympic sprinter.

On a clear night, over two thousand stars are visible to the naked eye.

It costs more to send a child to a reform school than it does to send one to Eton.

23 December

The richest ten per cent of the French people are approximately fifty times better-off than the poorest ten per cent.

The juke-box derives its name from the old English word for dancing – to 'jouk'.

The Chinese used fingerprints as a method of identification as far back as AD 700.

24 December

A large meteorite fell in Leicestershire on 24 December 1965. Weighing over one hundred pounds, it is probably the largest to have fallen in Britain in modern times.

It is a criminal offence to drive around in a dirty car in Russia.

There are about twenty-three million cats in the USA.

25 December

The great film comedian W. C. Fields died on Christmas Day in 1946. His tombstone bore the words: 'On the whole I would rather be in Philadelphia.'

Vampire bats can hear sound frequencies which are over eight times higher than any picked up by the human ear.

26 December

Mao Tse-Tung, the first Chairman of the Chinese Communist Party, was born today in 1893. Before his rise to power, he was Assistant Librarian at the University of Peking.

There is a village near the Somme in France which is simply called Y.

27 December

Marlene Dietrich was born today in 1901. She was one of the most popular film actresses of her day and once said: 'Most women set out to try to change a man and when they have changed him they do not like him.'

There are more living organisms on the skin of a single human than there are human beings on the surface of the earth.

28 December

Maurice Ravel, the French composer, died on this day in 1937. He suffered from a brain disease late in his life, which left him unable to speak or even sign his own name.

Crocodiles are responsible for over a thousand deaths a year by the banks of the Nile.

In China, birthdays are usually celebrated only every ten years.

29 December

The Barbary apes in Gibraltar are well protected by the resident British. The tradition is that when the apes leave the Rock, it is a sign that the British will leave too.

The Tibetan mountain people use yaks' milk as their form of currency.

30 December

The Russian monk Rasputin was the victim of a series of murder attempts on this day in 1916. The assassins poisoned, shot, and stabbed him but they were unable to finish him off. Rasputin finally succumbed to the ice-cold waters of a river.

From the age of thirty, humans gradually begin to shrink in size.

31 December

'Bonnie Prince Charlie', the leader of the Jacobite rebellion to depose George II of England, was born today in 1720. Considered a great Scottish hero, he spent his final years as a drunkard in Rome.

The Anglo-Saxons believed Friday to be such an unlucky day that they slaughtered any child unfortunate enough to be born then.

Sharks' teeth are literally as hard as steel.

Index

Biography

Jan. 1, 4, 7, 10, 13, 19, 21, 22, 24, 28, 30 **Feb.** 3, 17, 19, 20, 21, 29 **March** 1, 3, 5, 7, 9, 12, 14, 15, 21, 22, 24, 31 **April** 1, 3, 4, 5, 8, 9, 10, 11, 12, 14, 27, 30 **May** 1, 3, 8, 13, 18, 29, 30 **June** 1, 2, 8, 11, 17, 19, 21, 23, 25, 27 **July** 4, 9, 11, 14, 15, 19, 21, 24, 25, 29, 30 **August** 1, 8, 10, 12, 21, 27, 30, 31 **Sept.** 3, 12, 16, 17, 25, 29 **Oct.** 7, 8, 10, 11, 12, 13, 14, 15, 17, 21, 22, 24, 26, 29, 31 **Nov.** 3, 7, 11, 12, 15, 19, 30 **Dec.** 2, 4, 7, 12, 14, 15, 17, 21, 26, 30, 31.

History

Jan. 1, 2, 5, 6, 9, 12, 15, 16, 17
Feb. 3, 5, 7, 9, 11, 12, 14, 16, 20 **March** 2, 8, 11, 13, 16, 17, 18, 19, 20, 23, 24, 25, 27, 30 **April** 1, 2, 9, 10, 11, 16, 19, 22, 23, 26, 30 **May** 2, 3, 5, 6, 12, 19, 20, 23, 24, 26, 27 **June** 4, 5, 12, 15, 16, 18, 20, 22, 26 **July** 3, 6, 10, 12, 19, 22, 25, 28, 30 **August** 2, 3, 4, 5, 6, 8, 11, 12, 15, 16, 17, 28 **Sept.** 1, 2, 6, 9, 10, 14, 15, 19, 22, 30 **Oct.** 4, 15, 17, 19, 21, 23, 25, 28 **Nov.** 1, 5, 10, 17, 20, 21, 22, 26 **Dec.** 4, 6, 7, 11, 14, 18, 23, 31.

Geography

Jan. 2, 4, 12, 13, 15, 16, 23, 26, 29 **Feb.** 2, 4, 13, 14, 18, 19, 20, 22, 23, 25, 26, 27, 28, 29 **March** 2, 7, 12, 20, 26, 27 **April** 3, 5, 9, 11, 12, 13, 16, 19, 22, **May** 2, 4, 10, 14, 16, 19, 22 **June** 5, 6, 7, 18, 19, 20, 29 **July** 1, 5, 7, 8, 10, 13, 18, 20, 22, 23, 28 **August** 2, 4, 10, 14, 15, 16, 18, 19, 28 **Sept.** 3, 8, 17, 18, 20, 23, 27, 30 **Oct.** 3, 5, 12, 13, 14, 15, 18, 20, 22, 27, 28 **Nov.** 3, 9, 12, 19, 24, 25 **Dec.** 1, 9, 13, 16, 24, 26, 28, 29.

Arts and Leisure

Jan. 2, 3, 6, 7, 8, 10, 11, 13, 14, 18, 20, 22, 23, 25, 31 **Feb.** 1, 3, 9, 10, 11, 12, 19, 21, 22, 23 **March** 4, 6, 10, 11, 16, 19, 21, 22, 23, 26, 31 **April** 3, 6, 15, 23, 24, 25, 27, 29 **May** 5, 8, 9, 10, 11, 14, 15, 16, 22, 23, 24, 25, 26, 31 **June** 1, 6, 7, 9, 10, 12, 13, 14, 17, 21, 23, 26 **July** 6, 8, 13, 15, 16, 17, 19, 20, 21, 24, 26, 27, 29, 31 **August** 1, 3, 5, 7, 9, 20, 22, 23, 25, 28, 29 **Sept.** 3, 4, 7, 8, 11, 12, 13, 18, 19, 21, 22, 24, 25 **Oct.** 1, 3, 4, 5, 6, 7, 9, 10, 11, 21, 23, 27, 30 **Nov.** 1, 4, 5, 8, 9, 10, 11, 13, 23, 25, 27 **Dec.** 1, 3, 5, 8, 9, 12, 13, 15, 19, 25, 27, 28.

Facts and Figures

Jan. 17, 20, 21, 22, 28, 29, 30, 31 **Feb.** 1, 4, 6, 7, 8, 16, 18 **March** 5, 6, 10, 13, 15, 23, 28, 29, 30 **April** 7, 8, 11, 13, 16, 17, 18, 20, 21, 28, 29 **May** 2, 4, 7, 9, 20, 26, 27, 28, 31 **June** 3, 4, 6, 11, 14, 16, 18, 27, 30 **July** 5, 6, 7, 9, 13, 16, 22, 31 **August** 3, 6, 9, 12, 13, 14, 15, 17, 18, 20, 21, 22, 24, 27, 30 **Sept.** 2, 6, 10, 11, 16, 23, 28, 29 **Oct.** 2, 4, 7, 8, 16, 18, 19, 24, 25, 27, 28, 29, 31 **Nov.** 1, 2, 6, 11, 14, 15, 18, 24, 26, 27 **Dec.** 2, 3, 6, 7, 10, 20, 22, 23.

Animal World

Jan. 4, 5, 8, 14, 15, 17, 19, 20, 21, 25, 26, 27, 28, 29, 30 **Feb.** 1, 2, 5, 6, 8, 11, 13, 14, 15, 16, 17, 21, 24, 25, 26, 28, 29 **March** 1, 3, 4, 5, 6, 12, 14, 17, 18, 19, 21, 28, 29, 31 **April** 2, 5, 6, 7, 25, 26, 30 **May** 7, 16, 21, 23, 28, 29, 30 **June** 2, 3, 9, 13, 15, 22, 23, 28, 29 **July** 2, 4, 12, 17, 18, 21, 24, 27 **August** 3, 4, 8, 11, 13, 19, 22, 23, 24, 26 **Sept.** 1, 4, 5, 11, 15, 19, 20, 21, 23, 25, 26, 28, 29 **Oct.** 1, 6, 8, 9, 11, 12, 15, 16, 20, 22, 24, 26 **Nov.** 2, 4, 6, 7, 12, 13, 17, 18, 23, 25 **Dec.** 2, 3, 5, 7, 8, 11, 16, 19, 20, 21, 22, 25, 28, 31.

Science and Nature

Jan. 3, 6, 9, 12, 19, 23, 24, 25, 26   **Feb.** 5, 8, 9, 10, 15, 17, 18, 22, 24, 25, 26   **March** 1, 2, 3, 6, 9, 13, 14, 17, 21, 24, 25, 26, 27   **April** 1, 2, 4, 6, 17, 18, 20, 21, 28   **May** 1, 6, 8, 10, 11, 12, 14, 17, 19, 21, 25   **June** 2, 8, 19, 24, 25, 29, 30   **July** 1, 2, 3, 4, 5, 7, 10, 11, 14, 15, 17, 20, 23, 25, 26, 29, 30   **August** 5, 6, 14, 16, 17, 18, 24, 26, 29, 31   **Sept.** 5, 14, 15, 16, 17, 19, 24, 26   **Oct.** 1, 2, 5, 9, 10, 13, 15, 16, 20, 23, 26, 30   **Nov.** 2, 3, 4, 6, 7, 8, 13, 15, 16, 17, 22, 24, 28, 29   **Dec.** 1, 5, 9, 11, 16, 17, 18, 19, 22, 27, 30.